FURNITURE MASTERPIECES
OF DUNCAN PHYFE

Warehouse, Salesrooms, and Workshop of
Duncan Phyfe,
at Nos. 168-170-172 Fulton Street, formerly
Partition Street

FURNITURE MASTERPIECES
OF DUNCAN PHYFE

BY

CHARLES OVER CORNELIUS

ASSISTANT CURATOR
DEPARTMENT OF DECORATIVE ARTS
METROPOLITAN MUSEUM OF ART

MEASURED DETAIL DRAWINGS
BY STANLEY J. ROWLAND
METROPOLITAN MUSEUM OF ART

PUBLISHED FOR
THE METROPOLITAN MUSEUM OF ART
BY
DOUBLEDAY, PAGE & COMPANY
GARDEN CITY   NEW YORK
1922

WILDSIDE PRESS

PRINTED IN THE UNITED STATES
AT
THE COUNTRY LIFE PRESS, GARDEN CITY, N. Y.

First Edition
after the printing of 150 de luxe copies

FOREWORD

Duncan Phyfe is the only early American cabinet-maker to whom a very large group of furniture may be attributed on documentary grounds. Much of the attribution to other American cabinet-makers is based upon purely circumstantial evidence, but in the case of Phyfe there exist documented examples of practically every type that is shown herewith. The aim, therefore, has been to present at least all the general known types of furniture from Phyfe's best period and as many variations of these types as space would permit.

It has also been attempted to place this art-craft of the Early Federal Period in the United States against the background of the time, thus to relate the utilitarian art to the influences—artistic, social, and economic—which controlled to a large degree the forms which it took.

The book has been a result of the assembling of material for an exhibition of the work of Duncan Phyfe at the Metropolitan Museum of Art in New York. In the search for Phyfe furniture there appeared a larger group of more varied material than had ever been supposed to exist.

It was deemed, therefore, advisable to put into permanent form this record of Phyfe's handiwork as it is known to-day, with no pretense to an exhaustive treatise. It may be affirmed that the book includes most of what is known about Phyfe and his work up to date, but the many surprising finds during the search for material to exhibit would lead any expert to speak with some hesitation in saying that all types or all variations of types of Phyfe furniture are included between these covers. At least those that are shown will form a valuable basis for future attribution.

The author's cordial thanks are due to those whose possessions are illustrated in the book. It is only their courtesy which has made possible its compilation. To these the author's appreciation is expressed: Mr. and Mrs. Warren B. Ashmead, Dr. and Mrs. Lewellys F. Barker, Mr. and Mrs. Harry H. Benkard, Mr. and Mrs. Allan B. A. Bradley, Mr. Henry de Forest Baldwin, Mr. Elihu Chauncey, The Colonial Dames of the State of New York, Mr. F. Kingsbury Curtis, Mr. and Mrs. Robert W. de Forest, Mr. and Mrs. Francis P. Garvan, Mr. and Mrs. R. T. H. Halsey, Mr. and Mrs. Herbert W. Johnston, Mr. and Mrs. V. Everit Macy, Mr. and Mrs. Howard Mansfield, Miss Jane Elizabeth Martin, Mr. and Mrs. Louis Guerineau Meyers, Mr. and Mrs. Henry Wilmerding Payne, Mr. I. N. Phelps Stokes, The New York Historical Society, The New York Public Library.

CONTENTS

LIST OF HALF-TONE ILLUSTRATIONS

LIST OF LINE DRAWINGS

FURNITURE MASTERPIECES
OF DUNCAN PHYFE

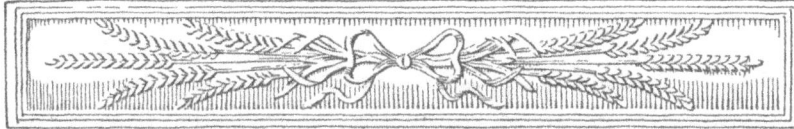

I

THE END OF KNICKERBOCKER NEW YORK

KNICKERBOCKER NEW YORK is gone! In the tall canyons
of lower Manhattan, few are the landmarks which recall to
us the little city whose more fashionable citizens drove on
bright spring afternoons to the pleasant country suburb of
Greenwich Village, doubtless relieved, good horsemen as
they were, that the hard paving of Broadway stopped at
City Hall! The residences of people of fashion were then
found on the Battery, while of the highest respectability
were lower Broadway, upper Pearl and Nassau streets,
Broad and Wall. Beyond the City Hall the softly rolling
landscape was ribboned with shady roads, flanked here and
there either by charming suburban homes to which the city
families retreated during the summer heat, or by tidy farms
whose owners were blissfully ignorant of eventual realty
values. Surely a provincial city but, none the less, developing more rapidly than it knew into a cosmopolitan one!

It was not until the very last years of its existence that
the consciousness of a Knickerbocker New York was formu-
lated into anything definite. The Dutch traditions which

1

had remained so important an element in the eighteenth-century town had hung about the city without occasioning any self-conscious attention or comment. It remained for a brilliant little group of young writers to utilize these traditions in their literary efforts and thus to preside in a two-fold capacity both as registrars of an epoch which was dying and as heralds of a new era which was just begun.

The first twenty-five years of the nineteenth century were marked in New York by an amazing activity which extended into all departments of human endeavour. There was a rapid acceleration of commercial growth which called forth a corresponding development of mechanical invention. A social consciousness was evolving from the compact society of a provincial city into the beginning of a cosmopolitan attitude toward local affairs. Civic improvements of surprising farsightedness were begun, and politics, both local and national, were hotly debated. The artistic expression of these contemporary interests kept equal pace. The artists who created and the patrons who supported the artistic achievements of the day were all in close touch with the life of the city in its various phases.

The result of this expansion of interests and activities was the rapid outgrowing of the Knickerbocker town both literally and figuratively. The very consciousness of the Knickerbocker tradition, for the first time definitely expressed, was in one way a romantic creation to which was lent the glamour of remoteness, and to which point was given by the survival up to date of many traits and customs of the early Dutch inhabitants.

It was at the beginning of this interesting and important

period that Duncan Phyfe came to live and ply his craft in
New York. His early struggles to find a foothold coincided
with the early years of the century, while the continually
increasing recognition of his sincere craftsmanship and consummate artistry kept pace with the changes in the city's
life and thought. His best work was done during this first
quarter of the century and constitutes an important record
of the cultural outlook of the people of the day. A brief
glance, therefore, at the New York of the time, the New York
which saw the accomplishment of Phyfe's finest work, will
give a necessary background against which to judge this
utilitarian art which served its purpose of contributing
largely to the creation of worthy standards of taste in the
public of the time.

By ten o'clock on the morning of the last day of the year
1799 a sombre throng of citizens had assembled in Broadway
near the triangular park which this thoroughfare formed
with Chatham and Chambers streets. A muted key was
set by the frequent signs of mourning visible throughout the
orderly crowd and was emphasized by the contrast with the
colours of the drooping flags, the brilliant hues of uniforms,
military and naval, and the shining insignia of the foreign
diplomats and their suites, the philanthropic societies, the
Masonic lodges, and the Society of the Cincinnati. In or-
dered ranks the cortège formed, each group falling into its
appointed place—citizens, foreigners of various nations,
representatives of the army, navy, and militia, of the civil
government, paternal and philanthropic societies, mercantile

groups, musical associations and clergy.   Near the end came
the great catafalque surmounted by the urn, glittering with
burnished gold, draped in black, and flanked by eight pall-
bearers.   Thus with pomp and ceremony was the funeral
of the great Washington commemorated by his fellow citizens of the country which he more than any one man had
helped to found, and of the city which for a short time was
its capital.

The bier, followed by the General's horse caparisoned in
black, and led by two negro grooms, passed down the east
side of the Common to the head of Beekman Street, thence
through Beekman and Pearl streets up Wall Street to the
Federal Hall.   It was here on the 30th of April, 1789, that
Washington had taken the oath of office as first President of
the United States, and in recognition of this fact a short
pause was made before the building.   Following Broad and
Beaver streets, it passed around the Bowling Green in front
of the Government House, which had been built in the expectation that New York would be the capital of the republic.   Through the double rows of the marchers the symbolic
urn was carried up Broadway and into St. Paul's Chapel,
where it was placed before the altar.   Solemn memorial
services were held, a funeral oration was delivered by Gou-
verneur Morris, and musical eulogies were chanted.   The
people dispersed to their homes, perhaps to discuss the great
works of the first President of the new republic, perhaps to
speculate upon the future of that republic in the new century
which was just beginning.

The death of Washington, practically coinciding as it did
with the opening of the new century, marked the end of one

period in the country's history and the beginning of a new. The trying years of war, the more trying years of the consolidation of independence won, were over. The Government of the United States of America was organized and founded upon a constitution. The time had come for the new country to try its mettle in competition with the great world without, no longer as a colonial possession, but as an independent nation conscious of its strength, the extent of which could be gauged only by its exercise.

The route followed by the marchers in the Memorial Parade may well be taken as a summary outline of the city as it was at the beginning of the nineteenth century. Carrying out in the main the lines of growth suggested by the old Dutch town, the lower end of Manhattan was divided by streets which followed generally the shore lines of the East and Hudson rivers and were intersected at irregular intervals by cross streets running from river to river. The present location of the City Hall, which was not yet begun, marked a northern limit to any real city development. There, on the "Common," stood the Bridewell, the City Alms House, and the Prison. Most of the country north of this point retained a purely rural aspect. Within easy reach was the Collect Pond around which youths and maidens sauntered on Sunday afternoons in summer or upon whose frozen surface they skated in winter. It was here in '96 or '97 that John Fitch had made his crude experiments in steam navigation. Other uptown resorts for pleasure were the Old Vauxhall at the corner of Warren and Greenwich streets, a house built by Sir Peter Warren and a public garden patterned after its famous London original, while various road houses along the East River offered in their menus tempting specialties to the summer boating expeditions and winter sleighing parties which came their way. In so small a town as this New York there was no exclusively residential section, but in all the streets the residence and the shop, the church, the tavern, and the market elbowed each other without giving or taking offence. The finest houses now being built of brick with slate roofs were on the Battery and in its immediate neighbourhood, lower Broadway and its intersecting side streets. Broadway was the Bond Street of New York and contained many fashionable and elegant shops. Already at this time New York had begun to feel itself the leading city of the eastern seaboard. Its location immediately rendered it the most important port for European import as well as the most central point for domestic export. Founded originally as a trading post—not as a haven for religious or political freedom—it was but natural that the commercial aspect of the city should always have assumed a preponderant place and that the marts of trade should have stood cheek by jowl with the church and the dwelling.

English though the city had been since the end of the seventeenth century, the Dutch tradition had been tenacious, particularly in the outlying country districts in New Jersey, up the Hudson, and on Long Island. In these districts the changes in tradition, in customs and usage, had come slowly, while in the city itself a much more rapid development had occurred due to the increasing number of immigrants from beyond the borders of the Low Countries. England preponderantly, of course, Ireland, Italy, and

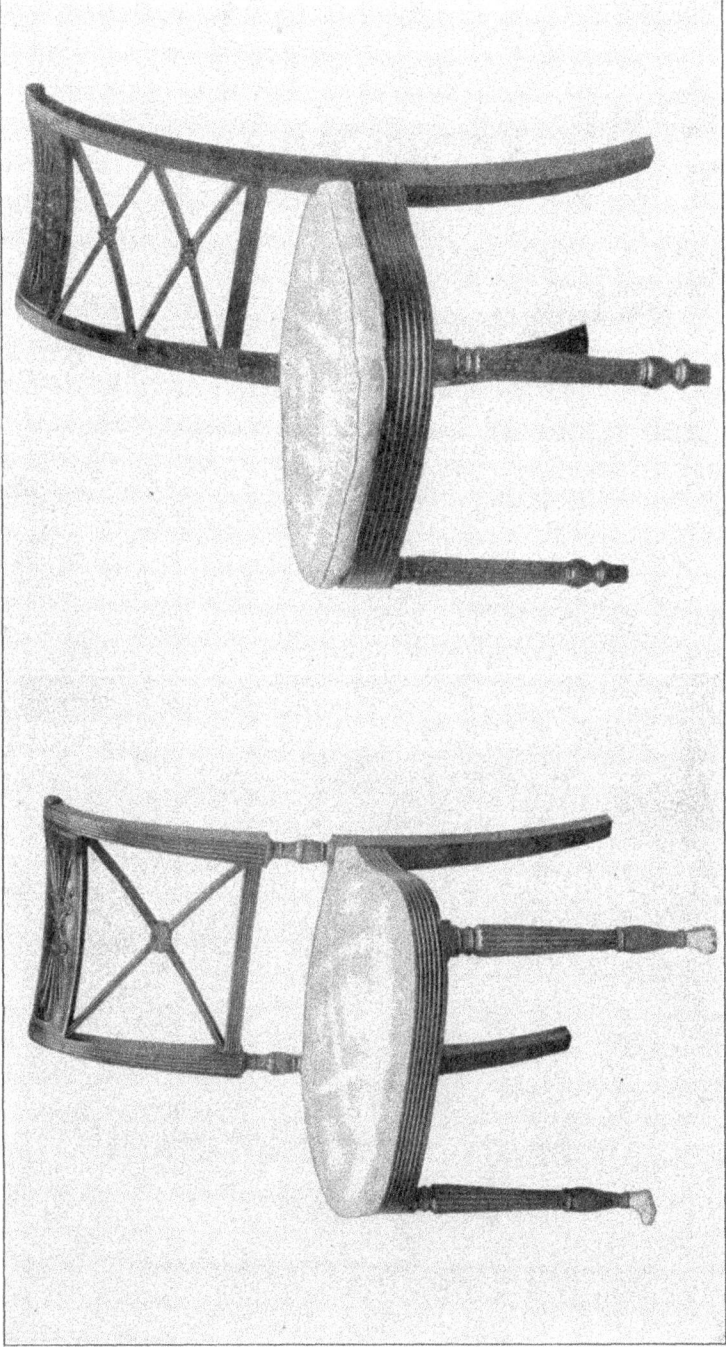

PLATE I. SIDE CHAIRS SHOWING SHERATON INFLUENCE

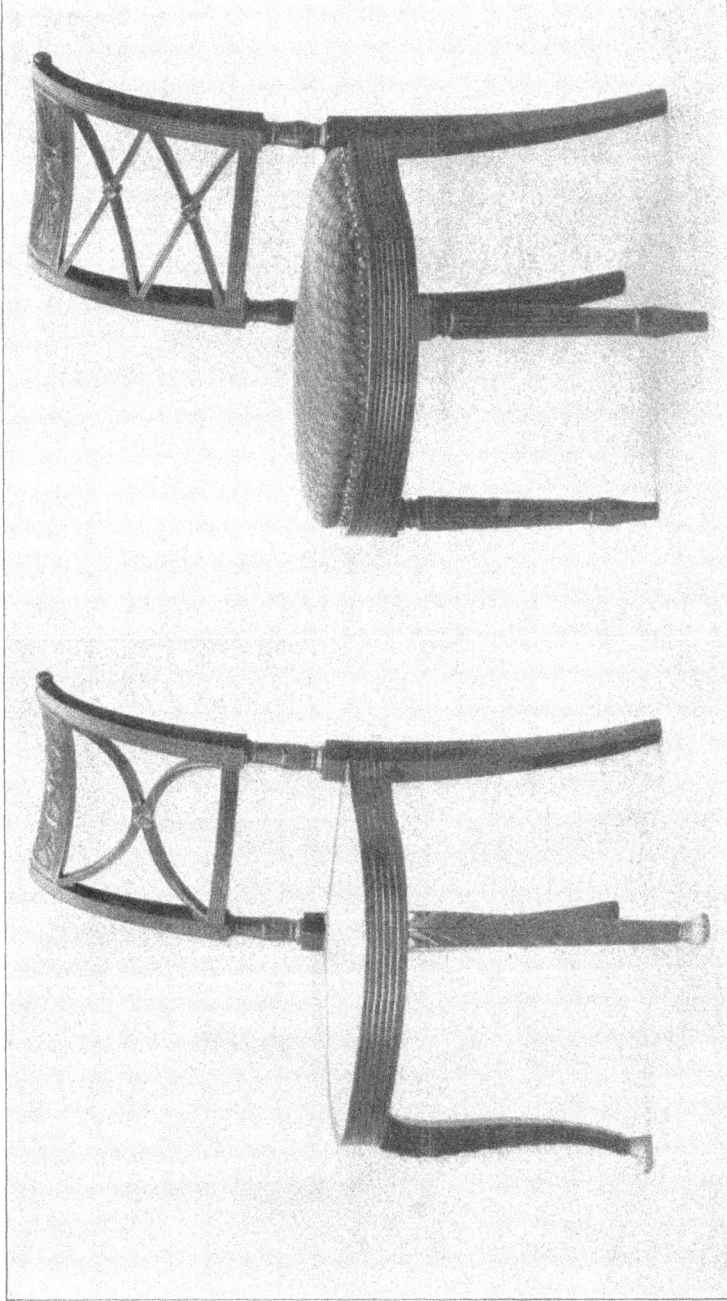

PLATE II. SIDE CHAIRS SHOWING SHERATON INFLUENCE

PLATE III.   ARMCHAIR, MATE TO SIDE CHAIR
PLATE II

PLATE IV. SIDE CHAIR WITH OAK-LEAF PANEL
SHERATON AND DIRECTOIRE INFLUENCES

France had all contributed to the growingly cosmopolitan population of the town. The French Revolution, with the resulting disorganization, led to a particularly large influx of cultivated Frenchmen. In numbers perhaps not greater than those of other nationalities which were coming at the same time, the conditions in France were such that the émigrés came almost wholly from the educated classes, members of the lesser nobility, and of the professional and artistic groups. It is not surprising, in view of this fact, that the influence of France and the civilization for which it stood—intensified by the memory of that country's aid to America in her dark hour—should have had a marked influence upon the city, particularly in its social and artistic life. The city's social history of the period is marked by a gradual change during twenty-five years from an English to a French flavour in which was mingled the faintest memory of the earlier Dutch characteristics.

Thus the original vigour of the city was reinforced by fresh infusions from abroad, in the repeated additions to its population of residents whose very presence in the new land argued their possession of sturdy bodies, active minds, and not a little imagination. All of this vigorous growth in population was paralleled by commercial prosperity, a proportionate increase in public and private wealth, a constantly widening horizon of political and cultural interests—in short, the beginnings of a cosmopolitan and somewhat self-conscious attitude toward the city itself and the world beyond its walls. Lengthy and detailed accounts of European affairs, predominantly the activities of Napoleon, fill large portions of the contemporary newspapers, as do the notices of arrival from and departures for Europe of those luxuries of fashionable life which each continent could offer to the other.

As though timed to guide the thought and influence the actions of the youthful city, so recently out of leading strings, there arose a constellation of literary stars whose effort was both to give to the city a background of recorded legendary or actual history and to mould its contemporary life by the exercise of gentle social satire. The brightest star of all was Washington Irving who, as a child of six, had with his nurse joined the crowd which gathered before Federal Hall when the oath of office was administered to the first President. Irving's studies for the bar had been interrupted by an illness which necessitated a voyage to Europe, whence he returned in February, 1806. He found the city at a pleasant moment in its growth with an organized and mellow society which afforded both a subject and an audience for the kindly wit and humour of his satire. Although admitted to the bar, his greater satisfaction lay in his literary activities, among the first results of which were the *Salmagundi* papers. Based upon the suggestions of Addison's *Spectator*, these essays were humorous satires upon the social foibles of the day and were written and published in conjunction with his brother, William, and James K. Paulding. His next effort, "A History of New York from the Beginning of the World to the End of the Dutch Dynasty by Diedrich Knickerbocker," was heralded by an advertising campaign of thoroughly twentieth-century character. In this history he not only satirized the pedantry of local antiquarians, but from the characteristics of the solid

Dutch burgher created a distinct literary type which later from time to time he developed in the charming stories of Knickerbocker legendary lore which have given to parts of the Hudson valley a permanent place in the literary geography of the world.

During a second lengthy sojourn abroad, Irving produced a number of exquisitely written stories and sketches upon English and continental themes which won for him his place among his European peers. Thus we see him not only as the creator of the first national literature based upon American incident but also as an author of international repute in the English reading world.

These youthful spirits, of whom Irving was the leader, contributed their share to the social life and literary activities of the town. Known as the Knickerbocker group, these young men divided their time between the city and a charming bachelor's hall, an old country home on the Passaic not far from Newark, celebrated in the *Salmagundi* papers as "Cockloft Hall." Of this lively group Mr. Hamilton Wright Mabie has drawn a vividly sympathetic picture in his little book, "The Writers of Knickerbocker New York."

During Irving's protracted sojourn abroad, the other members of this group of his friends and contemporaries were busy making names for themselves. James Kirke Paulding, best known as a political writer and anti-British patriot, wrote not only political treatises and satires but, as well, poems, novels, and parodies. He raised his protest against English dominance in political as well as in literary and artistic affairs. At the same time the two friends, Fitz-Green Halleck and Joseph Rodman Drake, were carrying on the impulse given by Irving and Paulding to social and political satire. Endowed, as Mr. Mabie says, with talent, though not with genius, these four "conspired against the dullness of the town and made it smile at its own follies."

In 1822 James Fenimore Cooper came to the metropolis, heralded by his reputation as the author of "The Pioneers" and "The Pilot." He was followed in 1825 by William Cullen Bryant, whose reputation as a poet was firmly based upon "Thanatopsis" and "Lines to a Waterfowl." Still attached to his career as a lawyer, it was some time before Bryant made his permanent connections as an editor. During the years 1821–1822, Richard Henry Dana 1st. edited in New York the short-lived magazine, *The Idle Man*. With his Bostonian background and his New York affiliations, he was a most important link between the literary groups of the two cities.

With the coming of these men and others toward the close of the first quarter of the century, the beginnings of a different school of writing were heralded. They are less a part of the last days of Knickerbocker New York than they are of nineteenth-century America, and they form a connecting link between a time which seems to us remote and a present which was, but just now, with us.

The artistic and intellectual interests of the town were nourished not only upon literary food. As a pendant to the group of writers, an equally vigorous company of artists and architects was working with a knowledge and sureness of touch which, while reflecting the changing tastes of the present, argued no lack of appreciation of the great traditions of the past. Here, too, we find men of versatile minds and training excelling not alone in one thing but in several, taking their places as active and conscientious citizens in the affairs of the city and the nation.

In February, 1801, there was opened in rooms in the Government House near the Battery an exhibition of paintings presented to the city by Napoleon Buonaparte, First Consul of the French through Robert Livingston, the Ambassador of the United States at Paris. To Chancellor Livingston, also, was due the establishment of the Academy of Arts which was formed by subscription in February, 1802, and reorganized in 1817 with Trumbull as president. As the Academy thrived, there were added to the collection "antique statues, busts, bas-reliefs, and books," among the last, twenty-four volumes of Piranesi, presented by Napoleon. Most of the "antique statues" were, to be sure, casts bearing such awe-inspiring names as Belvidere Apollo, the Venus of the Capitol, and the Laocoön. Of the "moderns" are mentioned busts of Washington, Hamilton, Clinton, West, and three of Napoleon.

Another popular resort for the artistically curious was John Vanderlyn's "Panoramic Rotunda." Here, on Chambers Street east of the City Hall, the well-known artist held an exhibition in a hall built for the purpose in 1818. The motley group of panoramic scenes included the Palace and Gardens of Versailles painted by Vanderlyn; the City of Paris by Barker; the City of Mexico, the Battle of Waterloo, and the City of Athens. A smaller connecting gallery was used by Mr. Vanderlyn to show his own paintings including his Caius Marius which had received a second prize at Paris.

Not far from the Rotunda on Broadway near the south

angle of the park was Mr. Paff's antiquity shop. He had no competitor in the fine arts of buying, selling, or repairing pictures. In the Architectural Rooms of Ithiel Towne and M. E. Thompson, in the Exchange, was assembled an extensive collection of books and prints relative to this noble art.

Of the painters whose names may fairly be associated with this period which we are reviewing, two are known to us chiefly by their artistic works, two by their scientific accomplishments.

John Vanderlyn and John Trumbull, historical, landscape, and portrait painters, ranked high as artists who painted in the taste and spirit of their time. Vanderlyn, a real Knickerbocker, born in Kingston-on-the-Hudson, studied, like the other painters of his generation, first in this country, then abroad. He was, in fact, the first American painter to study in France, rather than in England. His chief rival in New York, and by no means a friendly rival at that, was John Trumbull.

Trumbull, by the accident of birth, began his life with the advantages of good family and thorough education. His father was the Revolutionary Governor of Connecticut and Harvard was his college. In 1804 he came to New York with his English wife and set up his establishment in a house at the corner of Pine Street and Broadway. A good deal of an opportunist, he had made other visits to New York, usually, as now, in the effort to further his own success. His return found him well known as an historical and portrait painter, the pupil of Benjamin West, a soldier and a diplomat. He remained in America until 1808—the years from 1794 until 1806 had been prosperous but the embarrassments of commerce between 1806 and 1814 hit heavily the wealthy commercial clientèle of the painter. Again in 1816 he returned—the War of 1812 had come and gone while he was in the enemy's country—and his first effort was to revive the Academy of Arts of which he was elected president. From this time he was chiefly occupied in painting historical scenes for the Washington Capitol, then rebuilding. His relation to the Government was as nearly as possible that of a "court" painter. His work is a characteristic note upon the period, for it breathes the picturesque glory of battle, it depicts the important occasions in the foundation of the Government, and portrays the leading figures who took part in these events.

Robert Fulton and Samuel F. B. Morse are best known to us by their scientific contributions—Fulton for his successful forwarding of the use of steam in navigation, Morse as the inventor of the telegraph. But both of these men began life as painters and have left a number of examples of their work which bespeak their skill in an art which later was crowded out of their lives by scientific investigation.

Morse in 1824 was living in New York and was commissioned by the Corporation of the city to paint the portrait of the venerable Lafayette, who was then beginning his triumphant tour through the United States. Two years later he was instrumental in founding the National Academy of Design, of which he was the first president. This step brought about his ears the vituperations of the leaders in the Academy of Arts. For some years after this his painting and lecturing were continued before his inventions began to occupy all his energies. A charming fictional treatment of Morse's life is the delicate pen picture drawn in F. Hopkinson Smith's "The Fortunes of Oliver Horn."

Fulton, born in 1765, had practically given up portrait painting by 1794, according to Dunlap. His training had been similar to that of Trumbull and Morse. He had received instruction and encouragement from West in London, and had travelled on the Continent. It was during his residence in England, while he studied and painted, that he first became seriously interested in canal navigation and later, when an intimacy grew up between him and Chancellor Livingston in Paris, his dreams of the accomplishment of steam navigation had begun to come true.

Henry Inman, born in 1801, was one of the younger group of painters whose earlier work falls within our period. Apprenticed to John W. Jarvis at the age of fourteen, he was one of the organizers and the first vice-president of the National Academy of Design. Listed as a portraitist, he excelled both in miniature and oil painting, while in the latter medium his work included not only figure and portrait work, but genre and landscape as well. Inman's teacher and patron, Jarvis, was an eccentric soul who painted much and well both as a miniaturist and as a painter in oils. He not only worked in New York—with whose art, however, he is particularly associated—but travelled to Philadelphia, Baltimore, Charleston, and New Orleans to execute commissions for portraits.

Charles B.-J.-F. de Saint Mémin worked in New York from 1793 to 1798, returned in 1810 for a short time and again in 1812. A representative of the type of French artist who

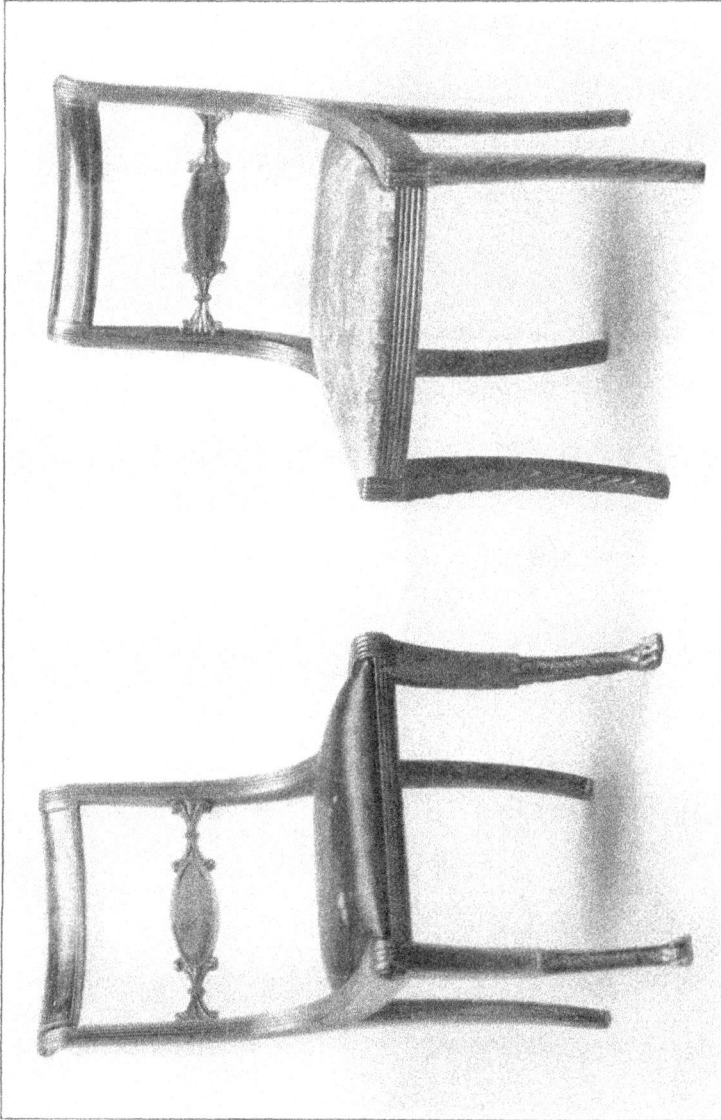

PLATE V. SLAT-BACK CHAIRS

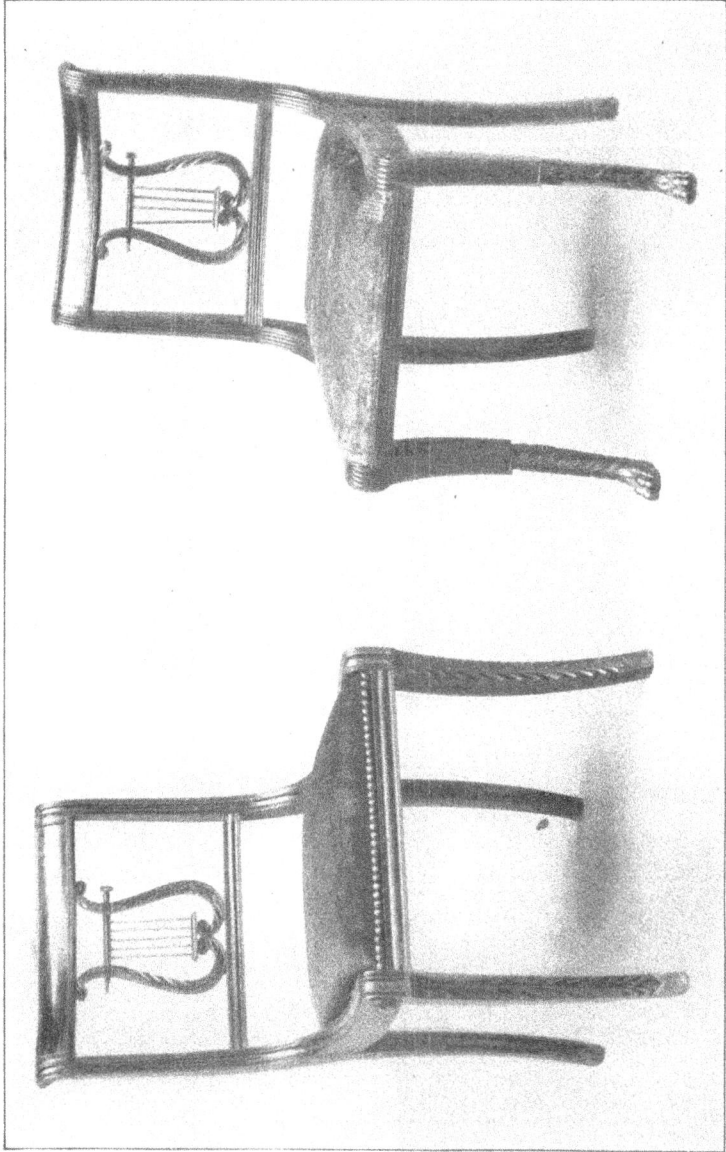

PLATE VI. LYRE-BACK CHAIRS

PLATE VII. ARMCHAIR OF DIRECTOIRE TYPE
CURLY MAHOGANY PANELS

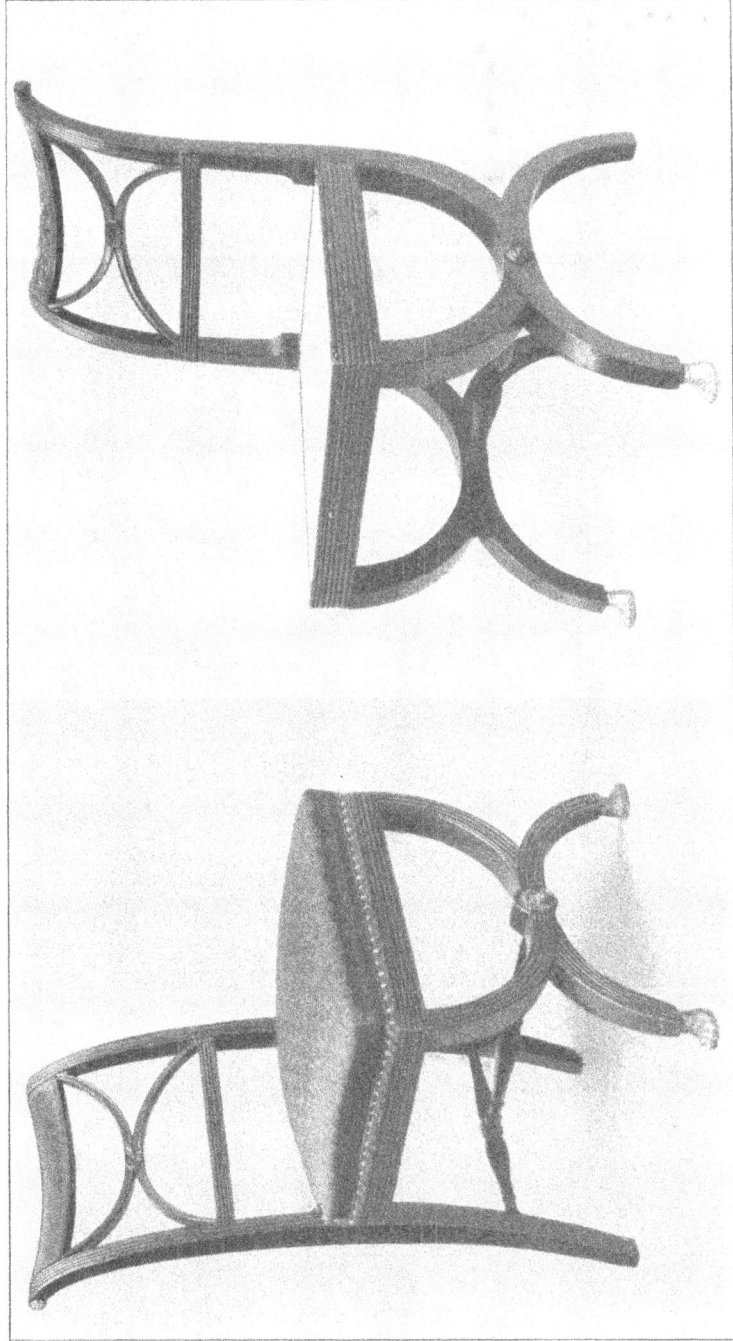

PLATE VIII. SIDE CHAIRS SHOWING EMPIRE INFLUENCE

came to this country after the Revolution in his own land, Saint Mémin engraved small medallion portraits of many of the most prominent people in the larger cities of the country. His technical method appealed to the spirit of the time. In executing his portraits, mostly in profile, he made a drawing which he reduced by pantograph to the small dimensions of his medallion. The copper plate was then engraved and the original drawing, life-sized in crayon, the engraved plate, and twelve proofs printed from it, were delivered to the sitter for the sum of thirty-three dollars! Saint Mémin's etched silhouettes are less well known than his engraved portrait medallions, but his views of New York are familiar to all interested in the earlier aspect of the city.

The work of these artists is a correct indication of the contemporary spirit. The chief works of each of them fall into one of the two groups of portrait or historical painting. The first group, that of portraits, was the inevitable result of a successful commercial era when fortunes were being made and families were assuming in their own eyes an importance which could well be expressed and perpetuated in this way. In the second group, that of historical paintings, the story of the founding of the republic is told in a familiar language full of pride in the bravery of its soldiers and the wisdom of its statesmen.

In a contemporary list of New York artists in which the names of Vanderlyn, Trumbull, and Morse occur, there are also mentioned the two architects, Thompson and Towne. To these must be added the name of John Macomb, the architect of the City Hall.

This building, the finest of its time in the city, if not in the United States, was begun in 1803. The premium for the best plan had been awarded to Macomb and Mangin, though there is still controversy as to how much credit is due to Mangin in the conception of the design. The prevalence of the yellow fever at the time of the laying of the cornerstone was something of a damper to the ardour of the citizens and was an accurate omen of the vicissitudes which were to beset the architect during the years before the completion of the building in 1812. The twenty-five thousand dollars voted in 1802 had been expanded to half a million by the time the building was finished. It is unnecessary to describe this little gem of early-nineteenth-century architecture for it may be visited any day in its present surroundings of skyscrapers. It is said that although the front and sides were built of Stockbridge marble, the north side was brownstone, painted, since it seemed hardly likely that any important development of the city would occur north of the City Hall Park! This story is not, however, consistent with the plan of the city as laid out by the commissioners in 1811, from which there has been but little deviation since. It would require much space to tell the story of the building of the new City Hall or to do justice to the professional ability and artistic genius of John Macomb. Let it suffice to put him at the head of the list of the New York architects of his day and to allow his masterpiece to speak for him.

Of the two architects Thompson and Towne, we have heard in connection with the library of architectural books, prints, and drawings which they had established. A surviving though dormant example of Thompson's work is the marble building which housed the U. S. Branch Bank in

Wall Street, where the new Assay Office now stands. This dignified façade, with its rusticated ground story supporting four Ionic columns, pediment, and entablature, will shortly be reërected in its permanent location as the south façade of the wing of American Decorative Arts at the Metropolitan Museum of Art. The material used was the marble of Westchester which was superseding the brown freestone of New Jersey and which was an adequate substitute for the fine marble brought at so great expense from Stockbridge, Massachusetts, for the City Hall.

Ithiel Towne was one of the more prominent architects of the city and possessed a very fine architectural library which was freely open to the use of students. Friend and associate both of A. J. Davis and M. E. Thompson, Towne designed and built many buildings both alone and in conjunction with Davis. Much of his surviving work is, however, an exponent of revival architecture, whether of the Greek or Gothic style, and falls just outside our period either in time or in spirit.

Thus the fine arts of painting, sculpture, architecture, and literature were not without representation in the early republican metropolis. Music and the theatre, too, enjoyed considerable favour. The Park Theatre in Chatham Street reigned supreme as the home of the drama and the opera. Gutted by fire in 1820, it was reopened on the first of August, 1821, to renewed glory, and was advertised as a fireproof structure to soothe the timorous! Traffic rules for approach to it by carriages were necessitated by the crush and confusion of vehicles bringing their fashionable fares.

A number of other theatres attempted to rival the Park,

but its fine location near the new City Hall and in the heart
of an exclusive district left it little to fear. An amusing
touch is seen in the rise from notoriety to gentility of The
Theatre, Chatham Street, not far from the Park. Originally somewhat *déclassée*, by 1824 it was considered a
"reputable theatre in every respect," perhaps owing to its
rebuilding and refurbishing in that year. Besides the three
established theatres running before 1825 there were many
other places of amusement, but none so attractive as Castle
Garden, the old fortress off the Battery, which had been rechristened for its mission of peace and pleasure. With the
covered amphitheatre surrounded by a broad promenade,
the lively band and the myriad twinkling lamps at night,
Castle Garden formed the most notable resort in the city
and was constantly thronged by a gayly dressed crowd in
all seasonable weathers, although its popularity with the
smart set fluctuated somewhat from year to year. Here
landed the distinguished visitor, Lafayette, in October, 1824,
to receive from the city the most spontaneous welcome it
has ever given to a foreign guest. The city papers were filled
with advertisements of dancing teachers—mostly with good
French names—and the terpsichorean art found many
devotees.

It is difficult to separate from the record of the artistic
growth of the city its contemporaneous commercial and civic
expansion. The mental picture of New York of this time is
a composite of pleasant social life and commercial activity,
of artistic effort and civic improvement, all interspersed with
timely political controversy. It includes the continued
stimulation of all of these by new inventions and far-reach-

ing plans for the future. Unfortunately, in a word picture it is impossible to unite all of these ideas so compactly, and almost equally difficult to condense into a few paragraphs the story of any one of the many departments of endeavour. Particularly is this true of the physical and commercial aspects of the city's growth which very closely reacted upon its artistic efforts, while the political questions of the day, centring very closely around parties dominated by the personalities of their leaders, are an excessively involved series of controversies which were the subject of heated dispute and personal antagonism.

The outside influences which acted most strikingly—and effectively—upon the city were those due to wars, fires, and pestilences. In some ways they hindered, in some ways helped, the city's expansion; certainly they all changed its geographical appearance. To wars and rumours of wars, to embargoes laid and lifted, were due the fluctuations of import and export which in large degree controlled the commercial prosperity and depression alternating in the records of customs revenue. Who would think of having his own or his wife's portrait painted or a new house built when the embargo was laying a lean hand upon every man's income?

During the early years of the century, the Napoleonic Wars occupied the stage of the world. The United States, a young but important maritime commercial nation, might well have been crushed between the upper and nether millstones, France and Britain. By turns and together these two nations flirted with or scowled at the young republic whose commerce was affected by the interference of French or British war legislation. The delicate situation resulting from this European condition, very complicated in detail, was resolved into actual war with England by the declaration of war in April, 1812.

The war found the country insecurely united as a political entity and considerably divided in its attitude toward the conflict itself. The general feeling in New York had been against war because of the interference with commerce, but when once the country was definitely involved, the city did not fall behind in its participation. Twenty-six privateers were fitted out at New York before October, volunteers were trained on land, large subscriptions to the war loan were obtained, and every effort was made to render the fortifications of the city adequate.

The city was the scene of several spectacular returns of war heroes. In September an enthusiastic reception was given to Commodore Hull of the U.S.S. *Constitution* after his defeat of H.M.S. *Guerrière* on August 19th. Captain Decatur sailed away from New York in his frigate, the *United States*, and returned in December the victor over H. M. frigate *Macedonian*, which he had disabled on October 25th by force of superior gunnery. A great banquet was given on December 29th for Decatur and Hull, both of whom had received the freedom of the city and had been asked to sit for their portraits which were to hang in the City Hall. The effect of these two naval victories did much to hearten the citizens by the proof of the prowess of the Americans when pitted against the greatest naval power of Europe.

Numerous other lesser naval victories were celebrated and land defeats mourned, but the climax of enthusiasm was reached in the illuminations and ceremonies in October,

1813, in honour of Perry's victory on Lake Erie in September. He, too, received the freedom of the city and his portrait was requested for the City Hall. Great rejoicing greeted the news of the signing of the treaty of peace in Ghent, which reached the city in February, 1815.

Fires, great and small, were of periodic occurrence in the town. The record of an extensive fire in an ancient section is usually followed by the projection of some fine stone or brick buildings soon to rise from the ashes. The yellow fever and other plagues which from time to time devastated the population were instrumental in extending the familiarity of the city dwellers to the delightful country near by. Greenwich Village grew into a thriving town during the epidemic of 1822. The disease appeared in Rector Street about the middle of July, and by the 20th of August practically all sorts of business offices were removed to Greenwich Village—even the ferries changed their courses—and scarcely any residents were left south of the City Hall. Early in November the citizens were able to return to their homes, leaving behind them, however, enough people to make up a nucleus for future growth.

Due to the desire partly to guard against the spread of disease, partly to simplify the topography of the city, very many changes and improvements were made in its geographical layout during the period. Whole streets in the old part of town were widened, Hudson and Washington Squares laid out, planted and surrounded by stately mansions. The triangle of ground, now Hanover Square, was cleared of its buildings and made a breathing space. A plan for the future development of the island was drawn up, the various fresh-water ponds were filled in, and the low rolling hills surrounding the Collect were levelled for filling.

At the same time these civic improvements were going on, the whole situation with reference to transportation was revolutionized by the application of steam to navigation. Fulton's successful establishment of steamboats on the Hudson was one of the most important events of the period in this country, if not in the world. The inventor's early death in 1815 prevented his witnessing the full development of the plans which he, with Robert Livingston, had inaugurated. By 1825, about one hundred steamboats of every description had been built in New York, passage to Albany was accomplished in ten to fifteen hours, the trip to England or France in about twenty-five days or a month. There were also lines to Vera Cruz, Savannah, Charleston, Mobile, New Orleans, Boston, Richmond, and Havana.

The establishment of these lines of steamship communication with European and American ports resulted in a huge increase both in the population of New York and in its commerce. The population in 1800, about 60,489 inhabitants, had by 1825 reached 168,000, an average increase of about 4,000 a year. The value of merchandise passing through the port, in 1800 about fourteen million dollars, by 1825 was more than thirty-four millions. Marked downward fluctuations resulted from the embargoes of the Napoleonic Wars and from the War of 1812, while the too great revival of importation after the latter war led to a paralysis of domestic trade and manufacture which affected all classes of society.

By the year 1825, however, the process of stabilization had pretty well worked itself out. Most of the activities which

PLATE IX. ARMCHAIR SHOWING EMPIRE INFLUENCE.
PART OF SUITE WITH SOFA, PLATE XVII

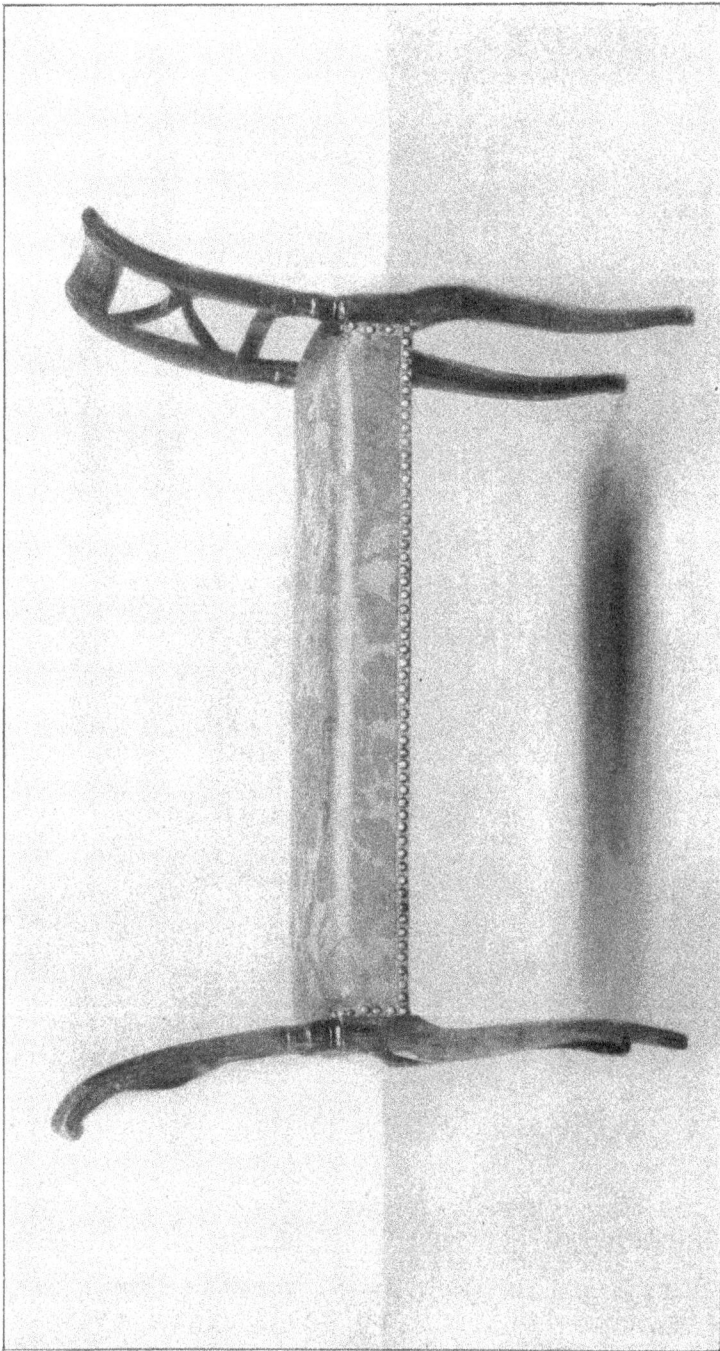

PLATE X. WINDOW BENCH, WITHOUT CARVING

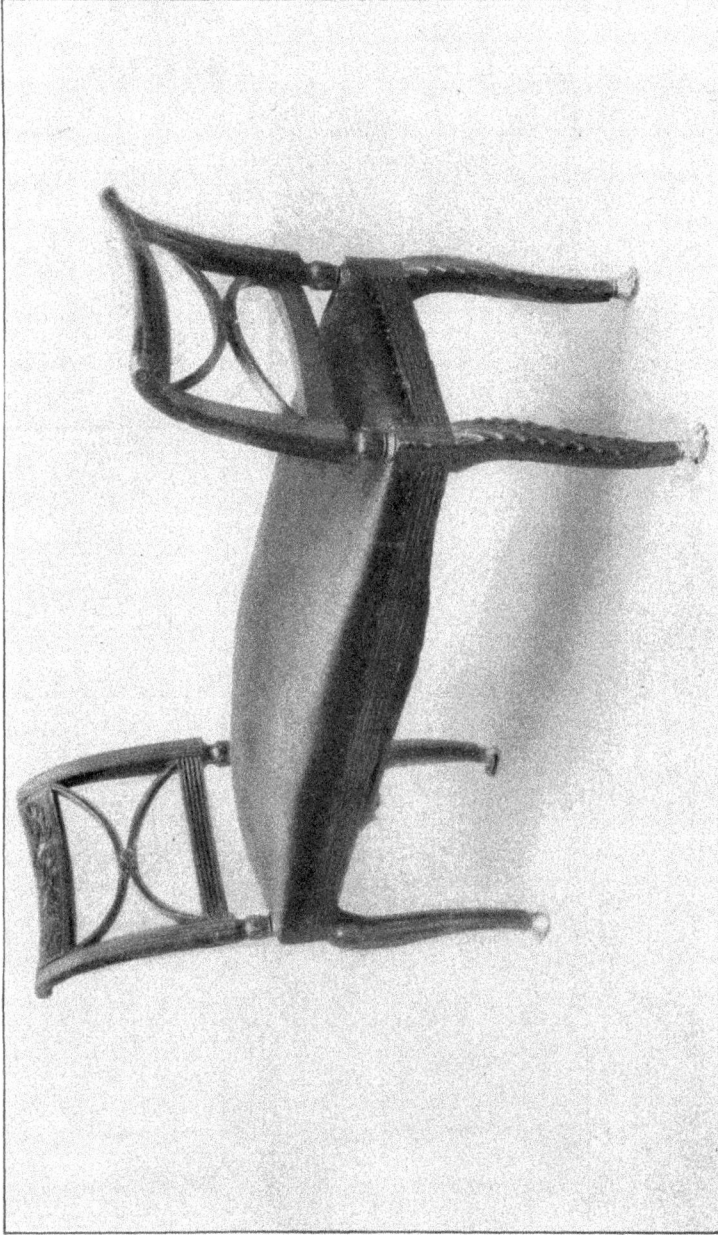

PLATE XI. WINDOW BENCH WITH CARVED LEAF PANELS AND ACANTHUS LEGS

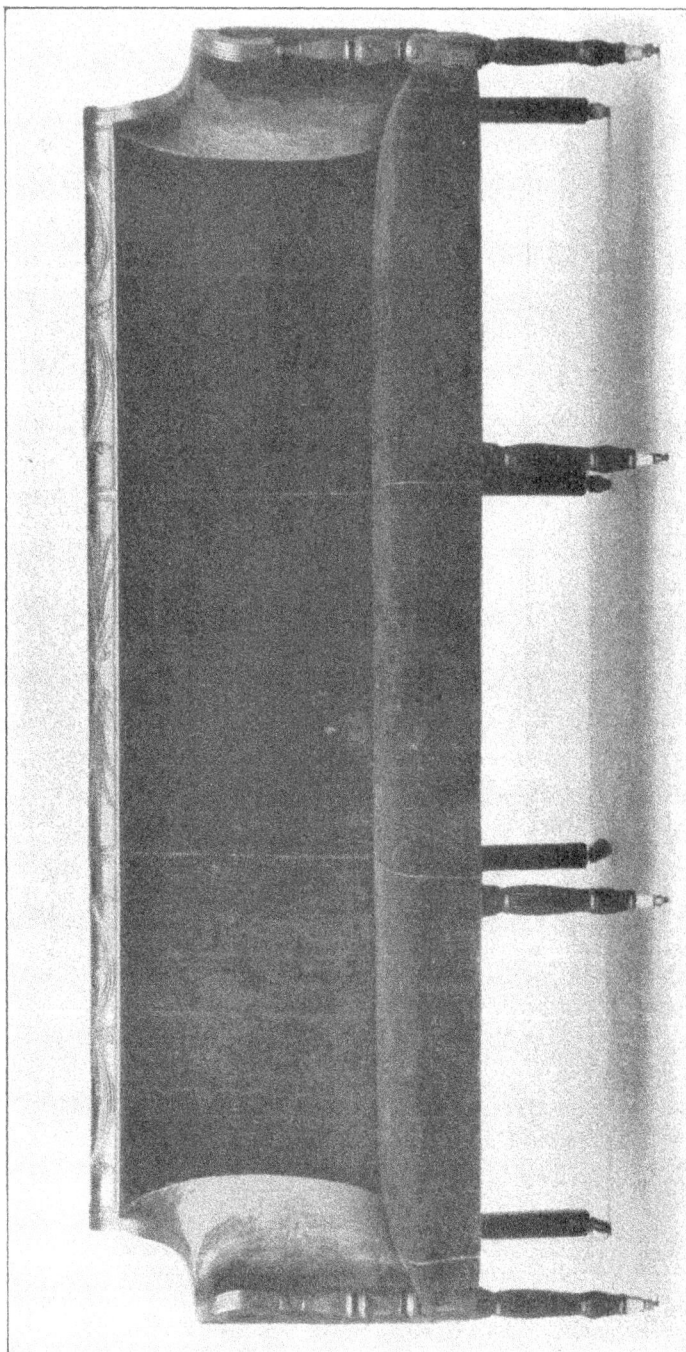

PLATE XII. SOFA, SHERATON INFLUENCE

have here been so briefly suggested were established in their regular courses. From the provincial city had evolved a young metropolis, filled with a considerable sense of its own importance, interested no longer exclusively in its own affairs but branching out in all directions to make valuable contacts with other parts of the country and with lands beyond the seas. The growth of New York had been more rapid than that of any other city on the eastern seaboard, and already through its port came and went a proportionately larger flow of export, import, and immigration. Its natural position rendered it particularly convenient as a centre of distribution for the rest of the country.

Transportation by land had not kept pace with transportation by water. The application of steam to navigation had given to the steamboat an advantage which it took the locomotive many years to discount, and even before the use of steam was thought of transport by water seemed far simpler than by land. Washington himself, before the Revolution, realized that if the great natural resources of the continent were to be deflected to the eastern seaboard, and away from the French province of Louisiana, served as it was by the Mississippi valley, some artery of transportation must be found between the region west of the Alleghanies and the Catskills. To him, the preferable route for this artery would lead into the Potomac. With a group of important Virginians, he had projected the building of a great canal between the Ohio and Potomac rivers. The site, which he later chose for the capital city, was thus, in his plan, destined to be near the metropolitan and commercial centre of the eastern coast, the great port of import from Europe and export from America. A fully organized company considered the scheme, surveys were made, capital was promised, and Washington was made president of the corporation for the development of the plan. Haste was desirable since there were already rumours of an important canal projected in northern New York State, to connect the Great Lakes with the Hudson River, though the British possession of Niagara was likely to give the proposed Ohio-Potomac canal a monopoly for some years.

Washington's election as President of the republic meant the relinquishment by him of all private business connections. He resigned from the canal organization, though never ceasing to give it his interest and to urge its construction as a vital step in the development of the country. But without his actual presence at the helm, the movement slowed down and finally was abandoned.

Washington's feeling that the unity of the country depended upon its being closely linked together by great converging highways was shared by other men of his day who, however, differed from him in their choice of location for the important seaport which was necessary as an outlet and a distributing point. As early as 1783 Washington and Governor George Clinton, on a trip to Saratoga Springs and through the Mohawk valley, had considered the feasibility of a canal from Oswego to Albany. Several other suggestions for canals in northern New York State to connect the Great Lakes with the Hudson were made from time to time, but it was not until 1810 that DeWitt Clinton, the great advocate of the Erie Canal, gave a fresh impetus to the movement. From that time until its final completion the sup-

porters of the project had to fight against the most bitter
opposition based both upon incredulity as to the practica-
bility of the canal and doubt of the capacity of the state
to furnish the means to complete it.

Begun on July 4, 1817, the work was finished in the au-
tumn of 1825. At ten o'clock in the morning of October
26th of that year the first canal boat, *Seneca Chief*, left Buffalo with a distinguished group of passengers. The event
was announced to the state by the booming of cannon from
one end of the canal at Buffalo to New York and back at
regularly timed intervals. On the 4th of November, the
Seneca Chief arrived at New York.

It was fitting that the city which had both originated and
supported the building of the Erie Canal from the beginning
should have led in the ceremonies attending its realization.
The event was celebrated in New York by extraordinary
civic and naval ceremonies and the enthusiasm of the people
reached a height seldom if ever attained before or since. The
celebration was in two parts, on sea and on land. The grand
fleet had arrived before sunrise on November 4th and the
day opened to the accompaniment of roaring cannon and
pealing bells. The *Washington* steamed down to welcome
the fleet, which was dressed in the brilliant flags appropriate
to the occasion. The naval procession filed past the Battery and was saluted by the military on Governor's Island
and in the forts at the Narrows. It then joined the U. S.
Schooner *Porpoise*, moored within Sandy Hook, where the
ceremony of the wedding of Lake Erie with the Atlantic was
to be performed.

A painted keg which had been made for the purpose and

filled with water from Lake Erie was emptied into the waters of the Atlantic by Governor Clinton, who delivered a short address.   In commingling the waters of the Atlantic with those of our Great Lakes, he said that he was thus commemorating the "wisdom, public spirit, and energy of the people of the State of New York" in establishing navigable communication between these two great bodies of water. Just before the ceremony the resolution was taken to preserve a portion of the water in bottles of American fabric, to enclose these in a handsome box made by Duncan Phyfe from a log of cedarwood brought from Lake Erie, and to send the case to Major-General Lafayette, so recently a visitor to the city.   After this impressive ceremony the vessels drew in to shore to witness the great land procession as it passed around the Battery.

This second part of the day's celebration was already under way.   The procession had formed under the direction of the Grand Marshal, on the west side of Greenwich Street with its right on Marketfield Street, and by eleven o'clock the line was already in motion.

The greatest land procession which had ever been seen in the city, this parade was arranged in four divisions.   Preceded by mounted trumpeters came the Grand Marshal of the day, General Augustus Fleming, with his four aides all mounted, uniformly dressed, wearing white satin collars and rosettes and carrying short white batons tipped with gold. These officials of the day were followed by the Corporation Band.

Following were the four divisions of marchers in whose ranks were represented all of the associations of crafts-

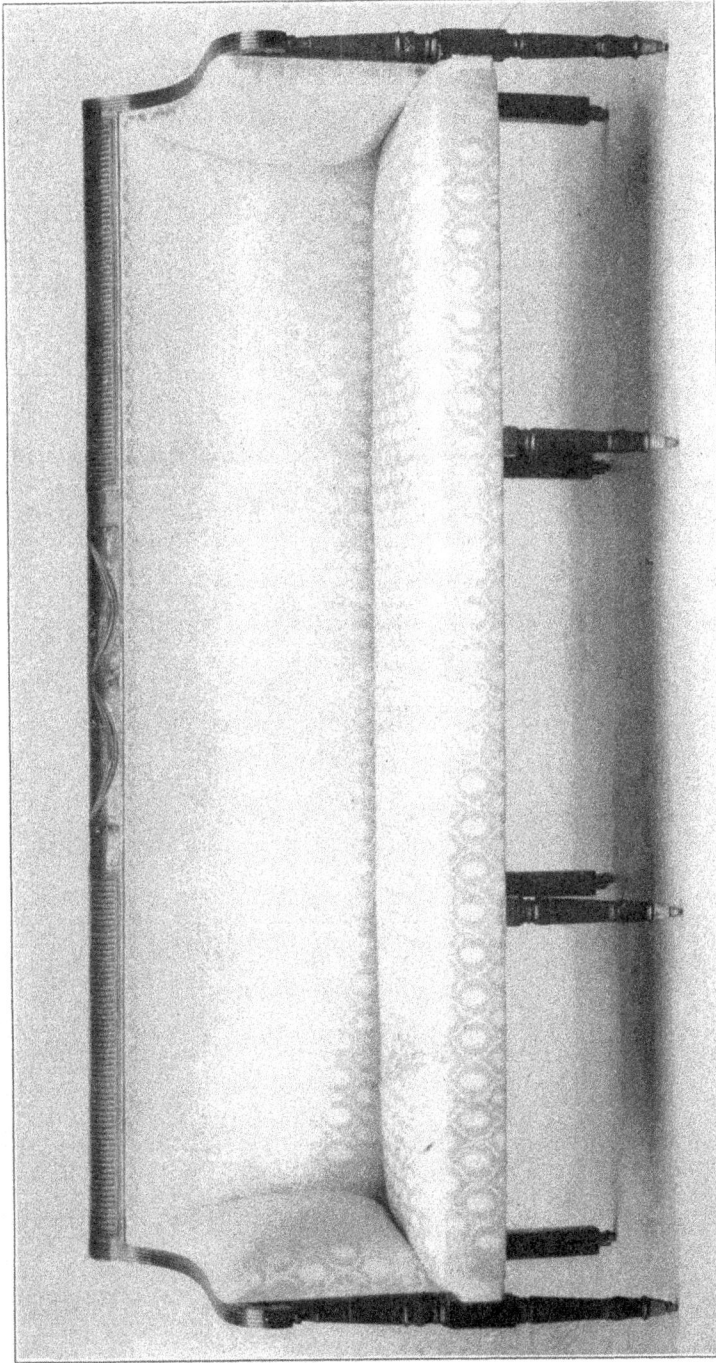

PLATE XIII. SOFA, SHERATON INFLUENCE

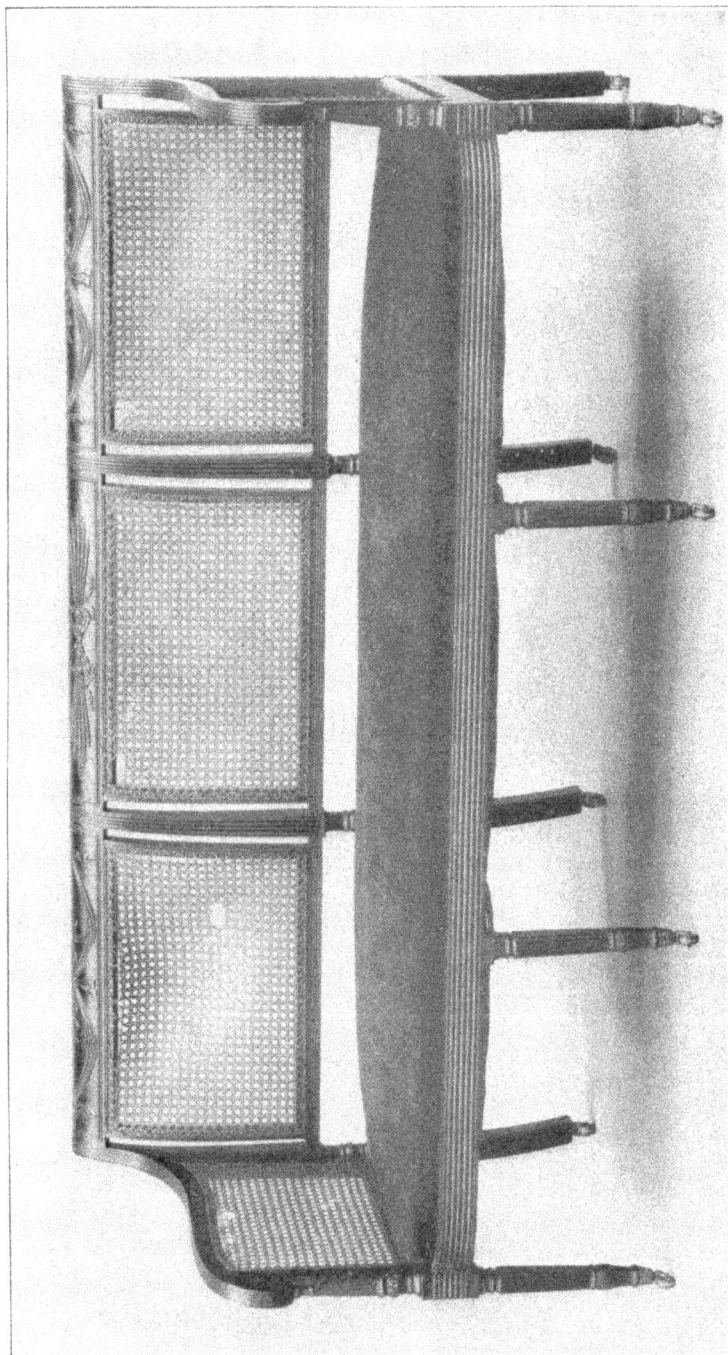

PLATE XIV. SOFA, SHERATON INFLUENCE

men, tradesmen, and mechanics, the fire department, students, officers of militia, and the Masonic lodges—in all, about seven thousand. Each of the thirty or more sections of the line was headed by a colourful banner painted with elaborate devices which in many cases was followed not only by marchers in ranks, but by large floats. The fire companies, particularly proud of their brilliantly painted engines, marched in high beaver hats and long-tailed broadcloth coats with the engines and implements of their calling tastefully (so the records tell us) decorated with paint, silks, and velvets. Some of the magnificent engines in their gaudy paint were mounted on floats that were covered with rich Brussels carpet!

Due to the nearness of Election Day, the assemblage of armed forces was forbidden, so that the parade represented purely the civic life of the city. The line of march led up Greenwich Street to Canal and Broadway, up Broadway to Broome Street, through Broome to the Bowery, and down the Bowery to Pearl and the Battery. The dazzling line reached the Battery about three o'clock, at which time, the aquatic part of the celebration having been completed, the vessels had drawn in close to shore. The procession passed around the broad walk at the edge of the Battery under the eyes of the notables on shipboard. As the end of the procession passed, the officials of the Corporation of the City disembarked with their invited guests and fell in at the rear, following all the way to the City Hall, where the procession dispersed.

This ended the festivities of the afternoon. In the evening the City Hall was illuminated by thousands of lamps and

candles and by a great display of fireworks. The next day
the chief guests were entertained on board the steamer
Chancellor Livingston, and on Monday, the seventh, the
whole series of festivities was concluded at a grand ball
given by the officers of the Militia.

In contrasting the two great parades, more than a quarter of a century apart—the one commemorating the death
of Washington, the other celebrating a great achievement—
we cannot fail to recognize vividly the changes which had
occurred in the city during twenty-five years. The different
lines of march of the two give some suggestion of the geographical expansion of the town. In the first, the groups of
marchers were formed on the basis of social cleavage; in the
second, chiefly on a basis of the various lines of human endeavour found in an active commercial community. There
is almost a suggestion of labour unions in the closely knit
groups of craftsmen and mechanics who rallied behind the
banners of their callings. Here is suggested a civic life
whose complexity required a definite grouping of its component parts—twenty-five years or more before one group
in the parade had been composed of "citizens" and included
all those who were not definitely allied with some one of the
military, philanthropic, or fraternal organizations. In the
celebration of 1825 there is seen a record of the scientific and
commercial advance of the years immediately preceding, the
shaping of a social structure which has continued to the
present day, and the consciousness of unbounded resources
in the newly accessible lands to the westward which were
now directly connected in a commercial way with all parts
of the globe.

The concomitant of this emphasis upon the scientific and commercial aspect of the city's growth was the decided lowering of the standards of taste in things artistic. Nothing more homely, nor at the same time more gaudily brilliant, than the preparations and decorations for the Erie Canal Celebration can be imagined as we compare them with the more distinguished efforts of an earlier generation.

The temporary death-knell of taste in the United States had been tolled, and the interest of the creative minds of the country was swinging away from æsthetic matters to those of scientific and commercial importance which were prescribed by the industrial revolution of the nineteenth century. Almost one hundred years after this interest seems to be swinging back to a normal position which includes in its scope both science and art, each with its proper emphasis in the sum total of cultural values. And the development of the æsthetic component of this modern culture must find its roots in a time when its standards were still high, its ideals still fine, and the integrity of its craftsmanship still unsullied by mechanical device.

II

DUNCAN PHYFE AND THE ARTISTIC
INFLUENCES OF HIS TIME

DUNCAN PHYFE (1768–1854) was born in the days of the great eighteenth-century furniture makers—in the Age of Cabinet-makers, as it has sometimes been called. In France, the reign of Louis XV and the Pompadour had seen the supremacy of the minor arts upheld by the great *ébénistes* and *cizeleurs*. These men enlisted the services of the most distinguished designers, painters, and sculptors of the day in the perfection and enrichment of the gorgeous furniture which filled the royal châteaux and those of the nobility. The craftsmen who later lent distinction to the work of the reign of Louis XVI, and of the post-revolutionary epochs of the Directory, the Consulate, and the Empire, were being trained in this school of noble design and of perfection in execution whose standards they carried on into the early nineteenth century. In England, Thomas Chippendale was at the height of his popularity and the designs in his "Gentleman and Cabinet Maker's Director" were still undisputed in their influence. Robert Adam, not long since returned from Italy, had already been appointed architect

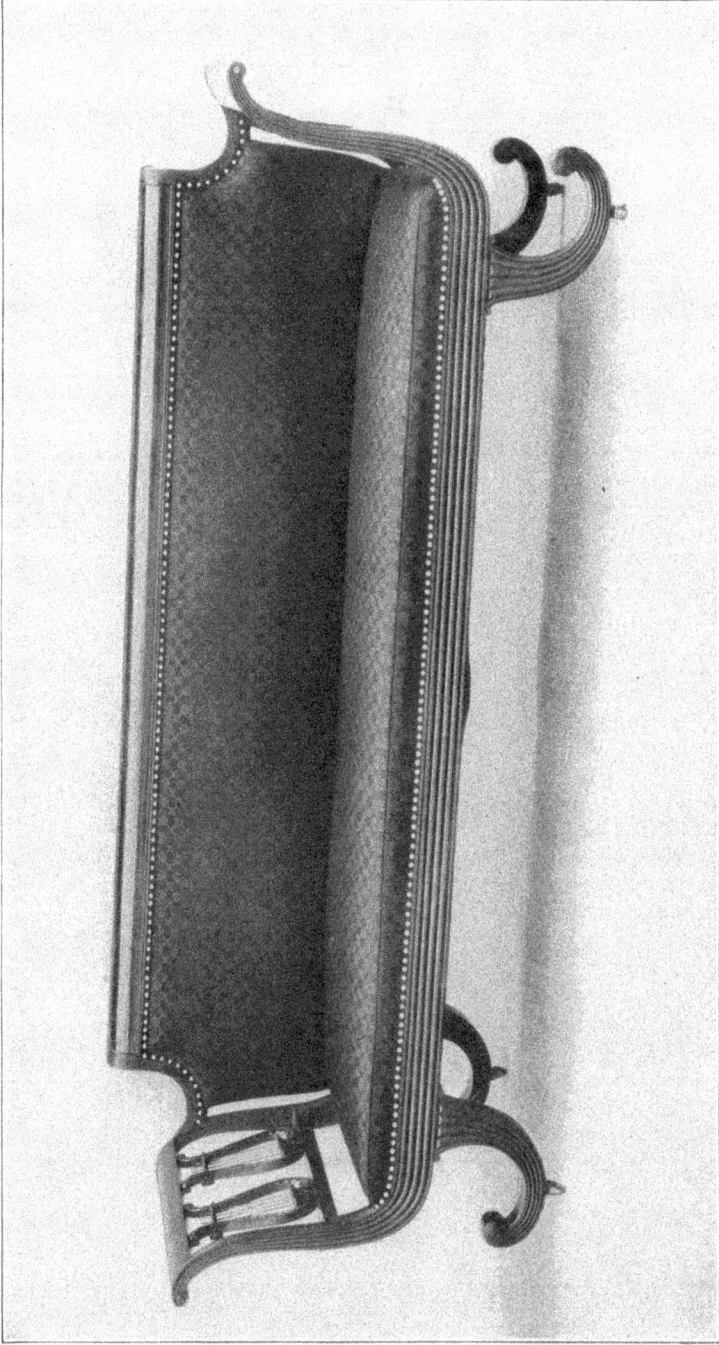

PLATE XV. SOFA, DIRECTOIRE INFLUENCE

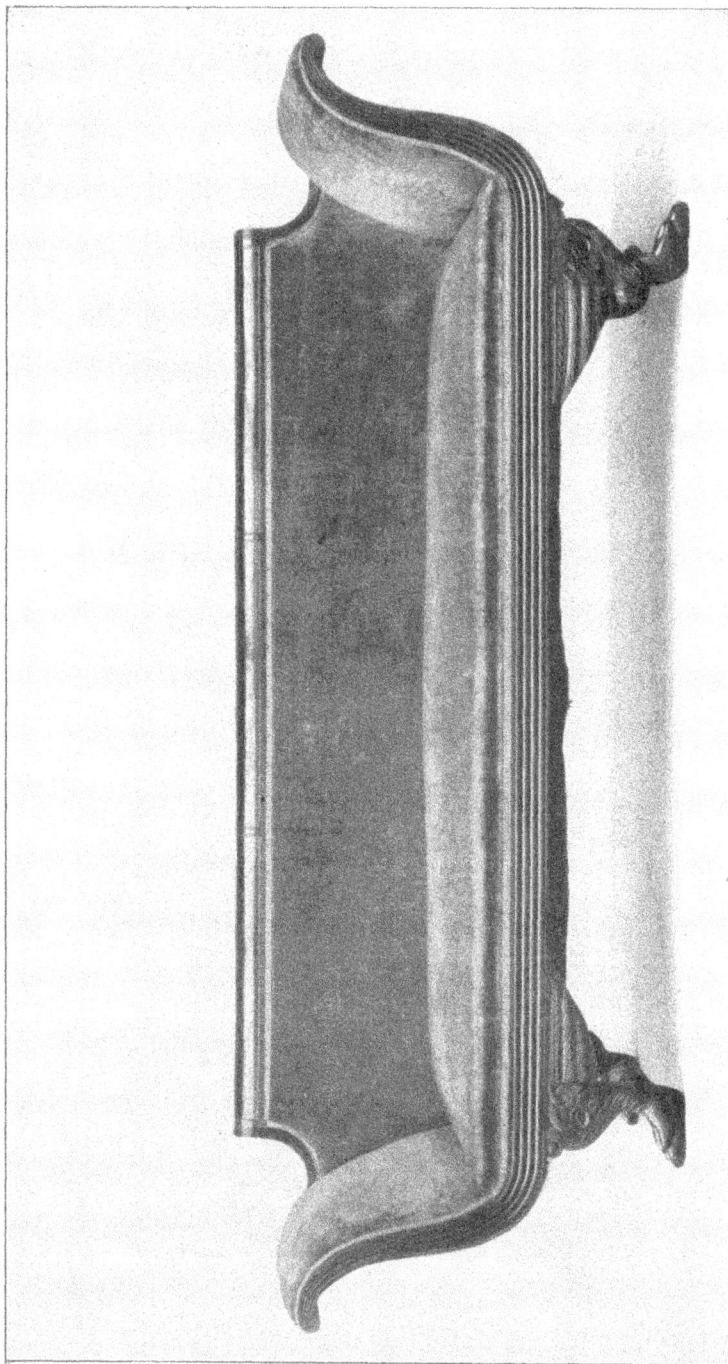

PLATE XVI. SOFA. DIRECTOIRE AND EMPIRE INFLUENCES

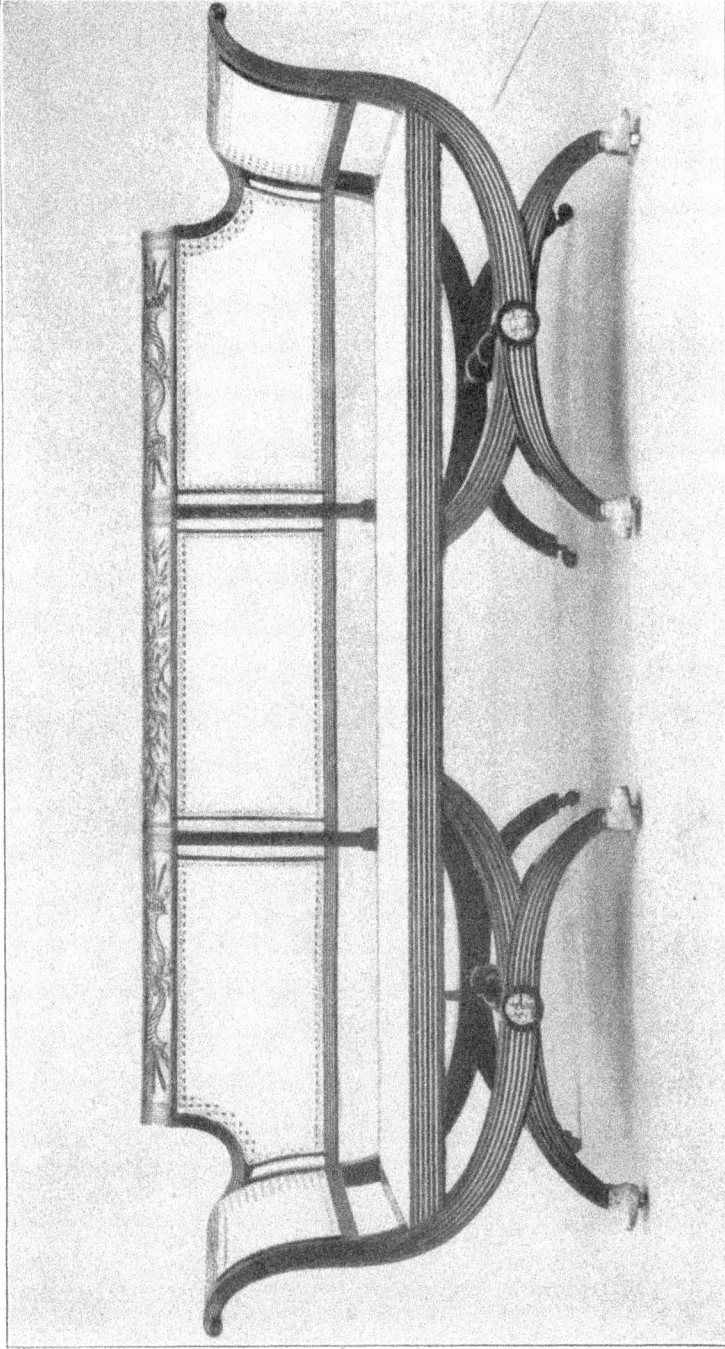

PLATE XVII. SOFA SHOWING DIRECTOIRE AND EMPIRE INFLUENCES

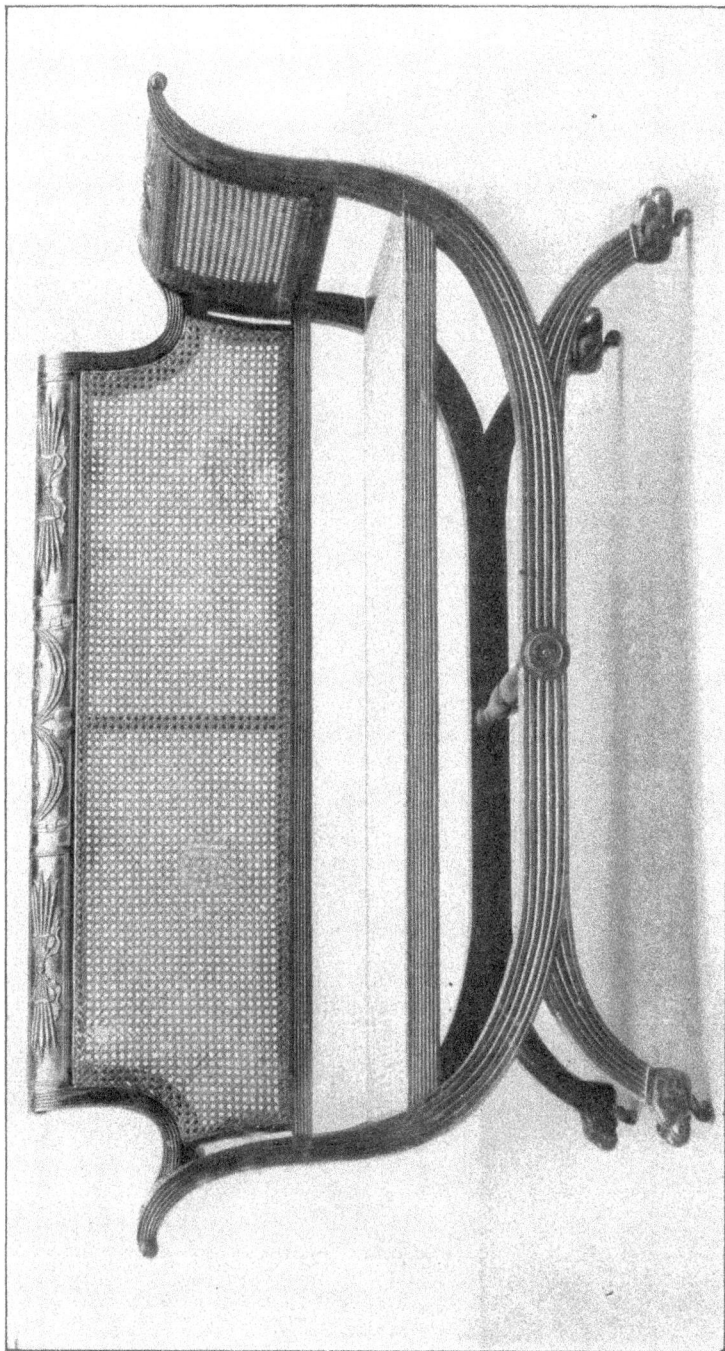

PLATE XVIII. SETTEE, EMPIRE LEGS AND CARVED PANELS, SIMILAR TO THOSE FOUND ON THE SHERATON TYPE OF SOFA

to the King and was soon to make his taste predominate over the elaboration of the Chippendale following. George Hepplewhite, whose influence upon Phyfe must be taken into account, was working at his trade and acquiring the experience in furniture design and construction of which the Hepplewhite "Guide" later gave ample evidence. Thomas Sheraton, Phyfe's immediate inspiration, then a youth apprenticed to a provincial craftsman, was imbibing a knowledge of the mechanics of his craft as well as formulating a complete conception of religious doctrine which bred in him the pedagogical instinct dictating the scope of his later activities.

This period at the end of the eighteenth century was one of sophistication and luxury, of a society interested chiefly in its pleasures which it took with an abandon outwardly elegant. The somewhat surfeited though ravenous taste of the moneyed classes needed the constant stimulation of variety or innovation. This led, in England, to a preponderantly eclectic character in utilitarian art, the art which responds most quickly of all to changes of taste or social usage, while in France the superior genius of the designers and craftsmen forced this eclecticism into moulds of their own conception.

The heritage of many epochs of furniture design which had come down to the cabinet-makers of the last half of the eighteenth century was brought by them to a luxuriant flowering. The evolution of furniture forms was already accomplished with a few exceptions which the usage of the time soon called into being. The wide variety of materials already in use left little scope to the inventiveness, in this line, of individual

workmen. The glossary of decorative motives was completed
by the introduction of the late Roman detail early in the
period. The remaining opportunities for the furniture designer and craftsman lay in his personal method of approach-
ing and treating his problems of design or in his originality in
combining his decorative motives and his rich materials. The
result of this condition of affairs was the conscious creation
of furniture styles which were differentiated each from the
other by a certain studied use of a limited number of decorative motives and design forms combined in characteristic
ways.

In the superb designs of the period of Louis XV, the ro-
caille taste which had been developing throughout the
seventeenth and early eighteenth centuries was brought
to its logical expression. It was a vehicle of perfect flexi-
bility for the rendition of the subtle, refined, and aristocratic
taste of the time. Elaborate, often gorgeous, the furniture
design possesses an intellectual quality which it is sometimes
difficult for the uninitiated to discover, but its presence definitely refutes the charge of superficiality which is often levelled against the decorative art of the Louis XV period.

With the classical influence exerted by the archæological
investigations in Italy and the handsome publications of
Piranesi, the developed style of Louis XVI is marked by
colder and less inspired qualities of design though it retains
the same high standards of craftsmanship in its execution.
The debacle of the Revolution brought with it the desire for
simplicity on the part of its protagonists whose taste ac-
cepted the style of Louis XVI, with which they were in some
degree familiar, but shorn of much of its more elaborate

decoration. The furniture of the period of the Directory, strikingly related to that of Phyfe, is of this sort and shows a frequent use of woods unpainted and ungilded, decorated with low relief carving and characterized by attenuated proportion. Under the Consulate, the same austerity of design is retained but acquires a more elaborate appliqué of decoration, while with the Empire came the full blare of gorgeous decorative treatment and an increasing solidity of form based upon architectural formulæ.

To trace a parallel course in England we must return to Chippendale's designs, which, supplemented by others of less well known men, had given expression to the rococo love for the unusual and the exotic, which dominated the complicated taste of the time. His style at its best and most typical was of a very high artistic quality, of imaginative and intellectual content, suited to its uses and carried out in appropriate material. Both the decoration and structural lines were plastic, essentially, but in the latter the feeling for the material was seldom violated.

As the freshness of the style began to wane the tendency toward over-elaboration made itself all too obvious. The bizarre and eccentric became the rule rather than the exception, and the effort degenerated into one of striving to produce the novel rather than the fine effect.

Due partially to this undesirable ingrowing tendency of the art itself, partially to the budding romanticism of the time, the innovations begun by Robert Adam in the third quarter of the eighteenth century met with hearty endorsement. The discovery and excavation of the ruins of Herculaneum and Pompeii had gripped both the scientific and romantic interests of the cultivated public, so that a contemporary architecture and decorative art referring directly back to those late-Roman times held an immense appeal for a considerable group of people. It was upon this basis, therefore, that Robert Adam built up the style to which his name is attached.

Although he was an architect, not a cabinet-maker, the necessity for suitable furniture in the houses which he designed—in which the prevailing style of Chippendale seemed to him out of place—soon led Adam into the designing of furniture and decorative accessories incorporating the motives which he had made his own. These included a classic symmetry in composition, the preferred use of the straight line in vertical structural members, and of geometrical forms, curved or polygonal, in plan. The total effect of these general changes was a lightening of the proportions, an interesting effect gained chiefly by the contrast of complementary forms and the employment of consistent scale, in an architectural sense, throughout the design. This definite scale in the furniture was emphasized by the use of much decoration of architectural origin. Vertical supports, such as table legs, were designed upon the basis of the classic fluted column. In carving were employed swags of flowers or drapery, acanthus, water and palm leaves, musical instruments tied with ribbons, and many other delicate details whose use was suggested by their former employment in architectural decoration. With Adam this type of furniture design resolved itself into that of architectural design in the small. The points of study were those of mass and proportion, the placing of decoration and, above all, correctness

PLATE XIX. CARD TABLE, SHERATON INFLUENCE
THE CORNER BLOCKS ARE CARVED WITH THE PRINCE OF
WALES FEATHERS

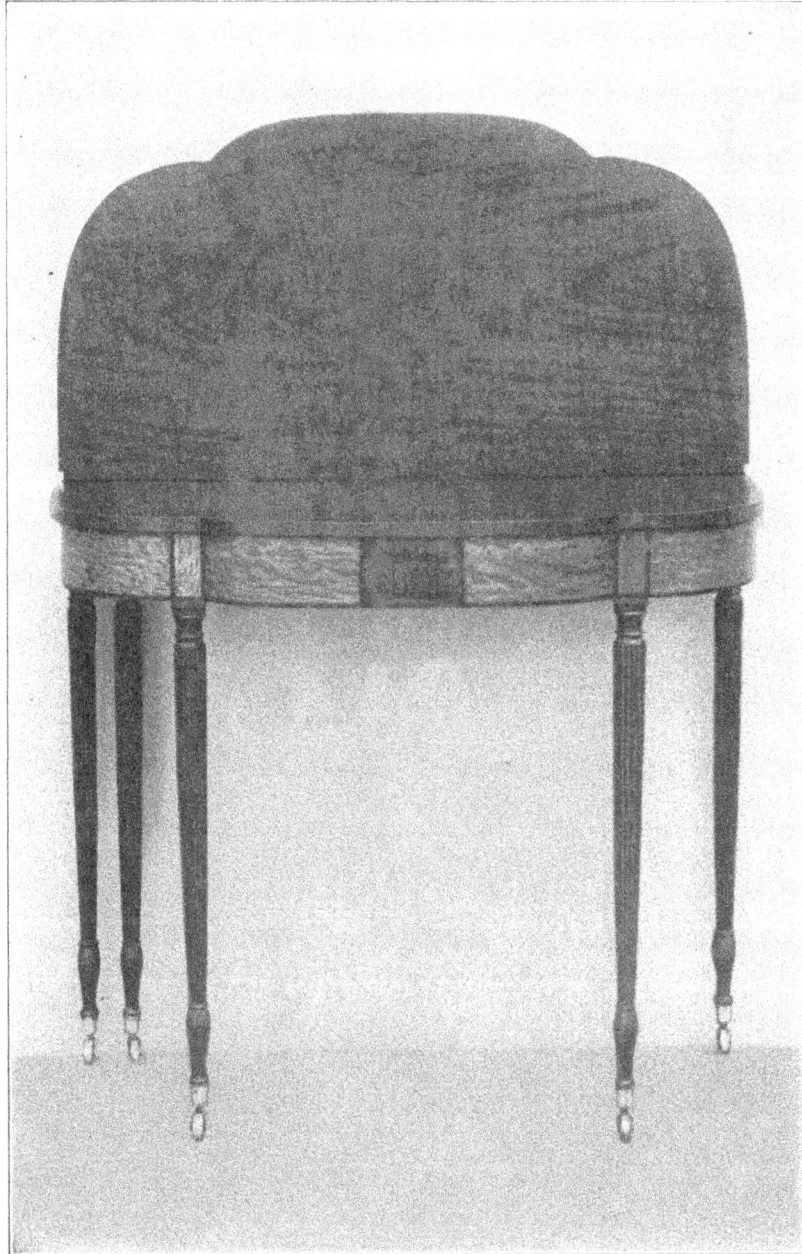

PLATE XX. CARD TABLE, SHERATON INFLUENCE

and consistency of scale. The most valid criticism of much
of the Adam work is levelled against the rather unimaginative and dry quality which results from this method of design creation.

Adam, as has been said, was not a cabinet-maker, and his
designs were, perforce, carried out by workmen over whom
he exercised some control. But at the hands of actual cabinet-makers, the type of furniture design begun by Adam
achieved its real perfection as an art-craft. The two names
of Hepplewhite and Sheraton stand out as characterizing
particularly personal treatments of furniture by trained cabinet-makers following out the impulse newly given by Adam.
Hepplewhite, like Chippendale in his last manner, had
turned to the France of Louis XV for the forms which might
possibly combat the rising tide of Roman detail that was
following in the wake of Robert Adam. Eventually he suc-
cumbed and we find him working in the pure Adam style
although imbuing his work with enough of his own person-
ality to mark in it a tendency away from Adam's artificiality
and toward greater comfort. In its final development, the
work of Hepplewhite shows the designer and the cabinet-
maker in him at complete harmony, confessing at the same
time obligations both to Rome and to France, but fusing
the two into an English whole under the fire of personal
enthusiasm for his craft.

In Sheraton is seen a cabinet-maker by trade and a designer by profession whose rank is among the foremost. He
figures not only in these two fields, designing and handi-
craft, but also as an editor and publisher of designs by other
men for furniture current in his time. Thus he stands as

one of the important educational influences in the art-crafts of the end of the eighteenth century, disseminating designs and information which came into the hands of practically every furniture craftsman to the lasting improvement of English cabinet-work.

Sheraton was not only a collector of other men's designs, but actually inaugurated a distinct style of his own which differed in many minute details from that of Hepplewhite. In his chairs, he showed genuine originality, although in much of his detail is seen a seasoning of the French style of the period of Louis XVI. All in all, his designs—for his actual handiwork is unknown and unidentified, and it is not believed that he ever did any cabinet-work after he came to London in 1790—are the very last word in fine cabinet-work of the eighteenth century in England, containing the essence of all the new ideas which had come into being in the last quarter of the century, as well as some of the tendencies which eventually led to its deterioration.

Phyfe, in America, was the heir of this age and helped to prolong it, in the new land, well into the nineteenth century. By the time that he was working entirely on his own responsibility, he was able to profit by all the accomplishments of the last great English cabinet-makers and, seeing their work as a whole, he could pick and choose those treatments which his native good taste and feeling for his craft told him were legitimate and appropriate for his use. At the same time the changing style in France was eventuating in the chaste simplicity of the Directory and the early Consulate, whose influences were felt very promptly in New York.

Born in 1768 at Loch Fannich, thirty miles from Inverness, Scotland, Duncan Phyfe came with his parents and their other children to America in 1783 or 1784. On the long voyage from Scotland two of the children of the family died, one of them his younger sister. The family settled in Albany, where the boy, Duncan, then sixteen years of age, worked at the cabinet-maker's trade into which it is probable that he had been inducted before he left home. After a time he went into business for himself in Albany, where it is said that he did considerable work before leaving that city. Sometime early in the 1790's he came to New York, lured, like many another ambitious youth, by the fame of the city as a growing metropolis which recently for a short time had been the capital of the country. Locating first in Broad Street, in the midst of a district full of cabinet-makers, he made several changes of abode and work, settling finally in 1795 in Partition Street, not far from the "Common." Here he stayed for the rest of his days, seeing the town grow far to the north and pass through many changes.

At first it was a hard struggle to get sufficient work, but a fortunate connection was made with certain members of the family of John Jacob Astor, whose wealth was already very great, and this led to more and more increased business among the people of means in the city. Even before 1800 it is probable that Phyfe's work was considered among the best obtainable in New York, for in at least one case we know of a man of wealth, who, marrying in 1797, had all of the furniture for his new home made by Phyfe.

The increasing prosperity of Phyfe coincided with that of

the city.   Many families, whose wealth was rapidly mount-
ing up, were building new brick or marble houses which had
to be furnished in the prevailing taste.   Many of them
found the furniture from Phyfe's workshop not only the
finest from the point of view of workmanship and design,
but best adapted to the character and scale of their interior
architecture.

His reputation, too, was spreading and orders came to
him from other cities, such as Philadelphia and Albany,
while in the adjacent country in New Jersey and the Hudson
valley handsome country seats were springing up and in
many of these his handiwork found a place.   To his shop
one could go not only for the exquisite mahogany drawing-room or dining-room suites, but, for the accommodation
of his clients, he would furnish kitchen furniture such as iron-
ing boards, clothes horses, pastry boards, and servants' beds.
He also did careful repairing of furniture.   This custom
was usual among the cabinet-makers of the eighteenth
century in England who undertook to furnish a house from
cellar to garret with appropriate articles.

That he very soon found business growing beyond his
expectation is proved by the increase in his property.   At
first with only the one house at No. 35, in 1807 he acquired
No. 34 next door, and in 1811, No. 33 Partition Street.   The
original house was still his dwelling with the salesrooms at
No. 34 and the workshop and warehouse at No. 33, these
buildings being all on the same side of the street.

Shortly after Robert Fulton's death, in 1815, measures
were taken to open through a street from the East River to
the North River to be called by his name.   About this time

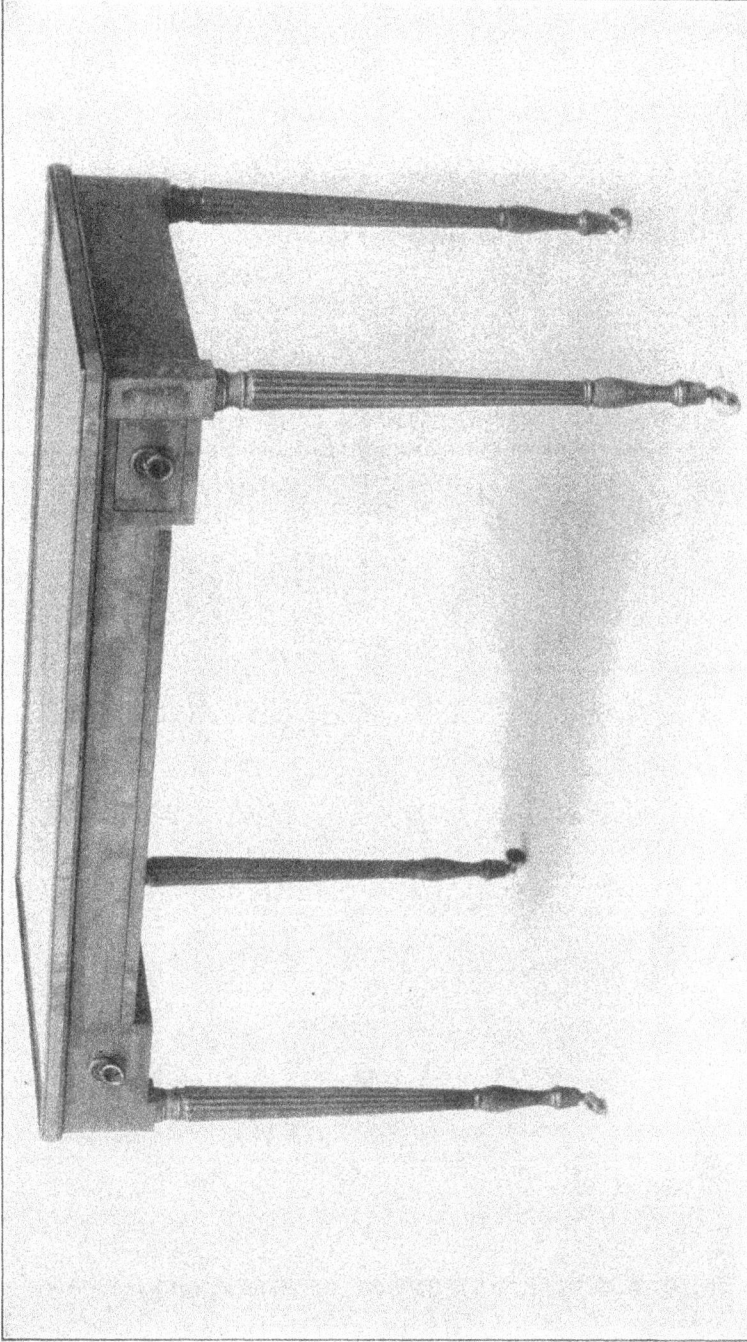

PLATE XXI. GAME TABLE, SHERATON INFLUENCE

PLATE XXII. PEMBROKE TABLE, SHERATON
INFLUENCE

PLATE XXIII. DROP-LEAF EXTENSION DINING-TABLE

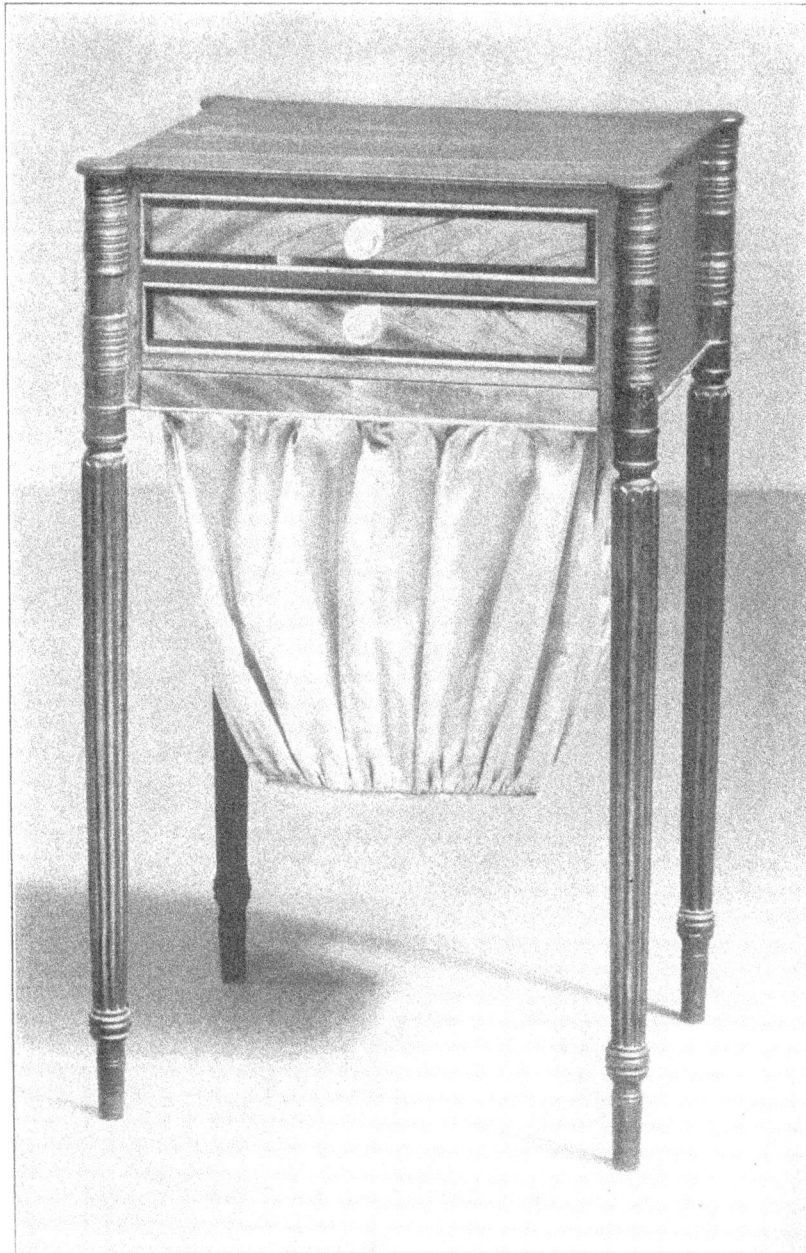

PLATE XXIV. SEWING STAND, SHERATON
INFLUENCE

Phyfe acquired the house directly across from his sales-shop, so that when, in 1816–1817, Partition and Fair streets, the same thoroughfare running east and west of Broadway, were rechristened Fulton Street, and the houses renumbered, Phyfe's addresses were Nos. 168, 170, and 172 with his house at No. 169 opposite. The frontispiece to this volume is from a contemporary view in water colour of the warehouse, workshop, and salesroom taken from the dwelling house. No. 172, originally the dwelling, brick with marble trimming, wrought-iron railing, and slate roof, is a typical house of the time, and was now used for warehouse purposes. The shop, with its show-windows and delicate architectural detail, is similar in style to many a design seen in the contemporary architectural books. In the original drawing the street number appears distinctly over its doorway, while modest signs over the show-windows bear the legend, "Duncan Phyfe, Cabinet-maker." The third building with its large windows was the workshop, though the dignity of its architecture would suggest a much more important usage. The old softly coloured drawing is a very charming example of architectural rendering of the period.

Mrs. Frances Trollope, visiting New York in 1829 or 1830, saw the houses practically as they were built and furnished between 1800 and 1825. She tells us that there were many extremely handsome dwellings on Broadway and in other parts of the town. According to her description, the drawing rooms were furnished with consummate taste, the floors heavily carpeted, the tables decorated with fine bits of porcelain and *objets d'art*, the walls hung with paintings. Even she, who viewed the United States through hostile eyes, was forced to admit the great beauty of the town and the taste of its inhabitants. More interesting still is her statement that French fashions absolutely prevailed, and that in walking down Broadway she could scarcely believe that she was not in a French town, as she noted the costumes of men and women and the gaiety of the shops. With this description in mind, we are not surprised to find the artistic influences of France equally conspicuous in the decorative art of the city. This unadulterated admiration of New York is of decided contrast to Mrs. Trollope's comment upon other places which she visited. The publication of her book caused, in the United States, such a furore of virtuous anger on the part of the Americans that international relations were actually strained. Her cold criticism of the country was scathing, and New York is almost the only city where she, a born cosmopolitan, seems to have felt enough at ease to have allowed her appreciation full rein. She does object to the omnibuses and their unmannerly occupants, but aside from these, the people and their homes seemed to her delightful.

Fulton Street by 1817 had become one of the main crosstown arteries of the city's traffic. At its western end were the landing stages of ferries to New Jersey and steamboats to Albany, at its eastern end the ferry to Brooklyn. The commercial advantage of such a location is obvious. Only one block from Broadway with its fashionable shops and smart dwellings, it was but a step from No. 170 Fulton Street to Paff's antiquity shop, where bric-à-brac or paintings could be chosen to combine with the rich mahogany of the furniture, or Vanderlyn's gallery visited to make arrangements for a portrait. Here, then, it was that Phyfe lived and worked, within a stone's throw of St. Paul's and almost within sight of the new City Hall, while before his eyes passed the varied pageant of the city's life, its parades, its fires and pestilences, its physical changes and growth.

The fashions of the day were too strong to be combated, and as the years went by Phyfe found it necessary to drift further and further away from the original distinction of style which had characterized his work. His earliest pieces, derived almost wholly from Hepplewhite and Sheraton, are worthy of a place beside any of their European contemporaries. The severe simplicity which was characteristic of much of it was not a sudden break from the simple but dignified furniture, Chippendale in origin, which was popular in the post-Revolutionary years of the eighteenth century. The influence of France, very strong in New York, and noticeable in costumes as well, led him early to adopt many motives of Directoire and Consulate origin, but he combined them skillfully with those of his earliest practice, still keeping the delicate scale and fine finish of the latter. As this French influence increased, the heavier forms of the French Empire came into vogue, and in response to the demands of his clients, by this time numerous, Phyfe was forced to enter into a style of work which was much inferior to that of his earlier days. Even this heavier work, with its use of gilt metal, is well made from a craftsman's point of view and possesses a certain character in spite of its over-solidity. The still further change which came with the dark ages of black walnut led him into the labyrinth of bad taste from which there was no egress.

In 1837 the firm name was changed to Duncan Phyfe and Sons, in 1840 to Duncan Phyfe and Son, and in 1847 he sold out and retired, to live on at his Fulton Street home until his death in 1854. Thus his life bridged the years between the last fine period of artistic effort and the collapse of taste which marked the nineteenth century, with all the political, social, and economic changes which this artistic transition signifies.

Although certainly holding an important position in the commercial life of his time, Phyfe, due to his retiring disposition, never took a prominent part in activities other than those connected with him in the most personal way. He seems to have led a quiet, God-fearing life, wholly occupied by his work and his family. All the recognition that he received, expressed in generous measure by his patrons, came to him by reason of his artistic and technical excellence. The only recorded official notice of his position as the leading cabinet-maker of his time is his employment in connection with the Erie Canal Celebration. In two commissions, he was called upon to undertake work which promised to be preserved among the memorials of that historic occasion. He made the handsome casket in which were contained the glass bottles, filled with water from Lake Erie, which were sent to Lafayette as a souvenir of this great event in the commercial history of New York. For the same occasion he made the handsome little cases in which the gold and silver medals, which were struck in commemoration, were enclosed and sent to the distinguished invited guests of the city and to the President and living ex-Presidents of the United States.

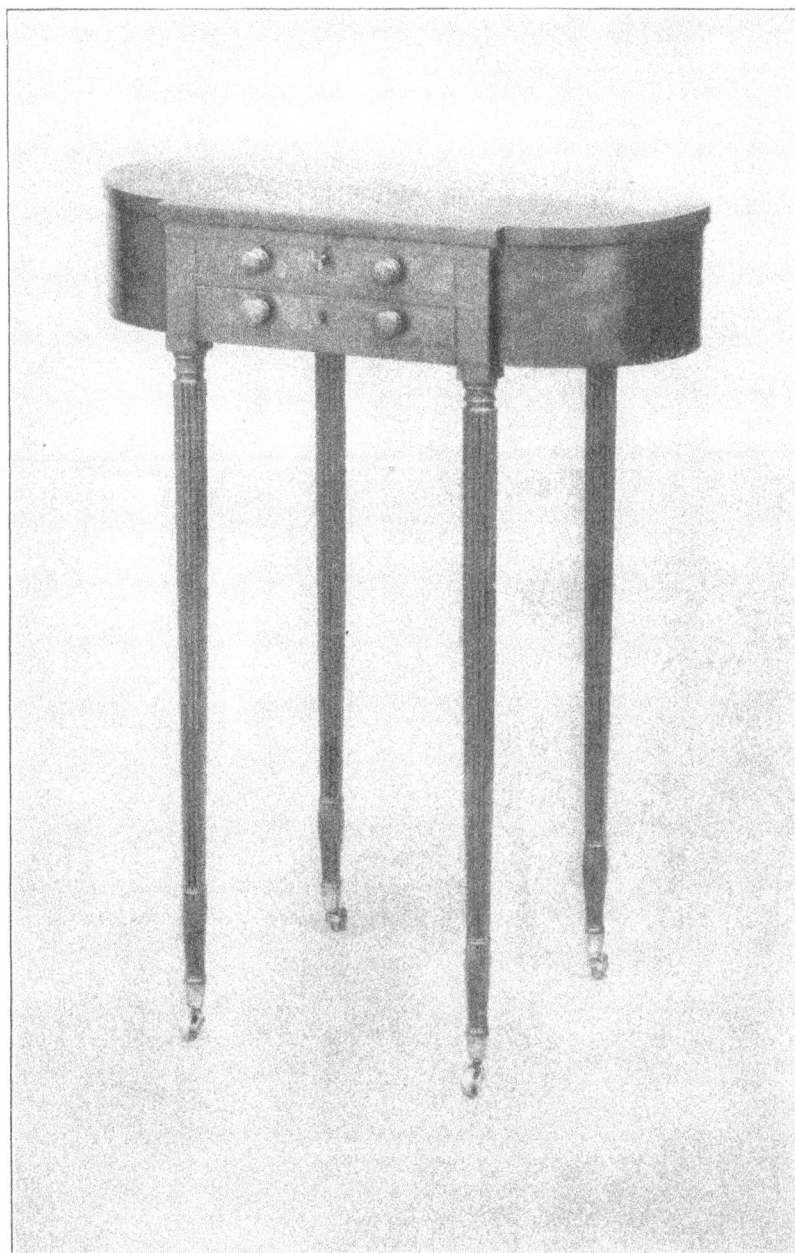

PLATE XXV. SEWING STAND. THE SILK BAG
IS MISSING

PLATE XXVI. SEWING STAND. THE SILK BAG
IS MISSING

The work of Phyfe, judged by the standards applicable to distinguished utilitarian art of all times, may be divided into four groups. The first and second of these, which include the work showing Hepplewhite and Sheraton influence and that in which the Sheraton and Directoire influences join, we may consider as a legitimate part of the history of furniture design. The second and third groups of the later American Empire furniture and of the black walnut "Butcher" furniture need not be considered as contributions of any value. It is with the first two groups only that we shall deal, dating as they do from the end of the eighteenth through the first quarter of the nineteenth century, and it is these which shall be considered in detail as their quality warrants.

By the time that Phyfe had become permanently established in New York as a cabinet-maker, all of the best books of furniture designs had found their way to the United States. Chippendale's "Director" must have been well known to him from his earliest days, if only as a curiosity of a superseded taste. At the time when he was first beginning work in New York, the Hepplewhite "Guide" and the Sheraton "Drawing Book" were being issued and must soon have appeared in the city. Certain of his work which we know was done in 1797 is completely Sheraton and most finished both in design and execution, while many of his details and methods of treatment are so closely allied to Hepplewhite that it seems reasonable to suppose that his very earliest work was based upon Hepplewhite models.

In discussing the furniture masterpieces of Duncan Phyfe it is not meant to suggest that every piece of what we call Phyfe furniture was made by his own hands. We are told that in his most successful latter years he employed more than a hundred journeyman cabinet-makers, turners, and carvers, and at this time it is highly probable that he did none of the actual work himself. But none the less, his was the directing mind, his were the designs, and his very close supervision stamped every piece with the refining mark of his criticism. Of the earliest work, much must actually have been made by him, and to some extent this may account for its close approach to perfection in its types, and the same, no doubt, is true of much of that work turned out before 1825.

The prices paid for Phyfe's work indicate that he was in a position to charge adequately for his furniture. These well-to-do people who were his patrons, recognizing the high quality of every piece which came from his shop, were willing to pay in full the fair price for his talents and labour. A bill rendered by Phyfe for furniture delivered to Charles N. Bancker, Esq., Philadelphia, may be quoted in full:

1816
Jany 4   Mr. Bancker
                                             to D. Phyfe dr.
To 12 Mahogany chairs @ $22 . . . . $264.00
    Sofa 122.00
    Piere table 265.00
    Pair card tables 130.00
    Packing 19.00
                                                   $800.00
             Discount 3 prct for cash . . . 24.00
                                              $756.00*

*It was well for Phyfe that Mr. Bancker did not pay his first bill promptly, since the mistake in subtraction would have cost the cabinet-maker twenty dollars.

2nd

1816

Jany 4	To 12 Mahogany chairs	$264.00
	" Sofa	122.00
	" Piere table	265.00
	" Pair card tables	130.00
	" 2 chairs	44.00
	" 2 pr. foot stools	30.00
	" Packing	2.00
		$857.00
	" do	19.00
		$876.00
	Cr. Stools	15.00
		$861.00

The value of the dollar of about this time was approximately the same as in our currency to-day, but the average fortune of the well-to-do man of those days would be a very small part of that of a man in the same position to-day. Therefore a sum of almost a thousand dollars was a fair amount to pay for enough furniture to furnish partially only two rooms, and the "Piere" table costing two hundred and sixty-five dollars must have been an imposing thing.

There is another little fragment preserved with this bill, although not a part of it. It shows two rough pencil sketches of chairs. One of them has a lyre back with dog feet and the top rail carved with cornucopiæ—a combination of motives unrepresented in any of the examples yet discovered. The second has the back made up of crossed curves, the top rail carved with leaves and the front legs in the Empire form of crossed reverse curves. The prices accompanying the first chair are as follows: cane bottoms,

$22, cushions $3, stuffed $23; for the second chair: cane bottoms $19, cushions extra $3, stuffed bottoms $21.

These show that our cabinet-maker had a regular scale of charges for each item which it is interesting to compare with those of an earlier day. In "The Journeyman Cabinet and Chairmakers' (New York) Book of Prices," published in 1796, are found itemized charges for every tiny detail of construction. On page 78 there are given prices for three types of chairs—an urn back, a vase back stay rail chair, and a square back chair. These approximate more closely in description than any others in the book to the types of chairs made by Phyfe. The average price for the labour on such a chair as one of Phyfe's simpler, carved slat sort would have been about fifteen shillings without any mention of carving on legs, slat, or upper back rail, and also exclusive of the cost of material.

With the question of Phyfe's style—its derivations from European sources and the amount of his own original contribution—it is better to deal in connection with the actual examples of his work, and this will be done in later chapters. The outstanding general consideration of his work as a whole is the fact that he, as the artistic heir of the great English cabinet-makers of the eighteenth century, profited by all the results of their study and experience, appropriated from them—as they in their turn had taken from their predecessors and contemporaries—what methods and motives of construction and decoration appealed to him, and with this fund of the traditional elements of his art he created a style of his own, full of the spirit of his time, influenced under intelligent and loving control by con-

PLATE XXVII.   CONSOLE TABLE, URN PEDESTAL

PLATE XXVIII. TIP-TOP CANDLESTAND

PLATE XXIX. DROP-LEAF TABLE, URN PEDESTAL

PLATE XXX. SEWING AND WRITING STAND

temporary taste and usage. His achievement lies in thus carrying on the ancient tradition a step further than it had seemed destined to go, and in harmonizing it with the changing taste of early nineteenth-century New York.

By the same token, his importance to us to-day lies in the fact that in him came to an end this fine tradition which disappeared when the æsthetic interests of the civilized world suffered eclipse by the industrial revolution of the nineteenth century. For a forward movement in the art of cabinet-making, this period would seem to be the point of departure. Just as the architecture of the early republic marked the end of a great tradition to which it is not impossible to return, so this early republican furniture of Phyfe, which marked the end of a parallel tradition in decorative or utilitarian art, may well form a basis for further development, not by unimaginative reproduction, but by observing his method of study and work which is full of integrity and the finest ideals of the art and craft of furniture-making, based upon the traditions which had come down to him as the heir of the great cabinet-makers of the end of the eighteenth century.

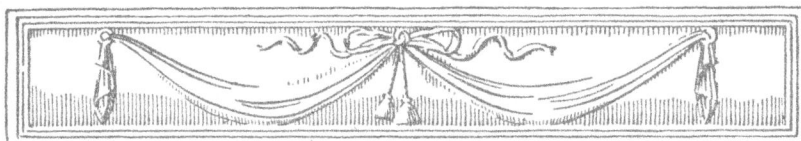

III

THE DISTINCTIVE QUALITY OF
DUNCAN PHYFE

THE distinctive quality of Duncan Phyfe, like that of the great eighteenth-century cabinet-makers, results from the combination of a number of elements which are treated in ways characteristic of his methods of design and execution. To arrive at a full appreciation of his work it is necessary to analyze the elements of his style, determining just what are their origins and how his use of them records his personal treatment in which his affection for his work and the consistency of his taste were the ultimate cohesives. Such an analysis holds also the suggestion of a way in which modern cabinet-makers and designers, basing their work upon traditional motives, of which Phyfe appropriated but a comparatively small number, may develop equally personal styles of their own.

Phyfe, for several reasons, is the only early American cabinet-maker to whom may be definitely attributed a large group of pieces. To Savery of Philadelphia and to Goddard in Rhode Island, the attribution of a number of pieces is made upon the basis of similarity to one or two authentically

48

documented examples of their work. To Phyfe, however, a very large number of documented articles of furniture are ascribed, and such attribution is strengthened by a very marked consistency of important characteristics.

The elements of Phyfe's style fall into two groups. The first of these is the furniture design as a whole, its proportion and line. Both of these are strikingly characteristic. The second element is that of the decoration which he employed, a characteristic second in importance only to the general design as a guide for the amateur to identify Phyfe furniture. Less important are the materials used and the furniture forms themselves. A review of these elements will show that there is a consistent feeling for certain proportional relations and certain combinations of line; that the decorative elements limited by taste are few in number but combined in many ways; that the furniture forms do not include every piece of furniture but are restricted to those which experience had shown could best be treated in the personal style which Phyfe was developing. The materials, too, which he used are carefully chosen for certain qualities of colour or texture which are maintained at the same high standard in most of his early work.

The analysis of his proportion is difficult. Its general effect is that of an exquisite balance between vertical and horizontal structural members. In his design one sees a very strong sense of structural integrity and economy in construction. In legs of tables, chairs, and sofas, the supporting effect is frequently emphasized by reeding or carving which carries the eye in the proper supporting directions up and down. These vertical supports are reduced to the smallest dimensions commensurate with complete stability, showing that economy of material which is indicative of the most developed forms of structural art. The horizontal elements, heavier, of necessity, than the vertical, are proportioned to the whole height of the piece in much the same manner as are the entablatures of the classic orders of architecture. Thus in a small card or console table the skirting is shallow, its lightness emphasized by veneered borders or tiny bead moulding at the bottom, its whole depth happily proportioned to the total height of the piece. In a library or dressing table—two variations of the same problem— where it is necessary for utilitarian reasons to introduce one or more drawers which require a deepening of the skirt, the supports are either made heavier, proportionately, or are coupled at the ends to suggest greater strength.

The proportions which Phyfe found pleasing in his earlier pieces are those suggested by the designs of Adam and carried on by Hepplewhite, Sheraton, and the French cabinet-makers of the Directory and the Consulate. Even more than do these, Phyfe observes integrity of structure based upon architectural lines, and his furniture shows fewer lapses from just proportional relations than that of his famous predecessors while confessing in many cases an increased lightness and refinement.

The structural curves which Phyfe employed show his real freedom in design. They are all fine, firm, freehand curves, which, while in many cases giving the effect of lightness, at the same time suggest adequate and solid support. His reverse curves, which occur both in chair and table legs, have as convincing a strength as any of the

PLATE XXXI. DINING-TABLE

PLATE XXXII. CARD TABLE WITHOUT SKIRTING

fine cabriole legs of the Chippendale period. The horizontal curves of table tops, chair seats, sofa seats and arms are often so slight as to escape detection, but they do add much to the flowing grace of the whole composition. One detail which is much remarked is the very subtle curve found on the longer centre leaf-portions of the so-called "clover-leaf" table top. (Plates XX and XXII.) Here it is found, by laying a straight edge along the edge of the table, that the long line, which appears to be straight, is in reality a gentle continuous curve. This is a feature not noted in any other American cabinet-maker's work of the period and may be taken as a Phyfe characteristic. None of his curves would seem to be geometrical. All appear to be free-hand lines based upon geometrical ones, but not drawn mechanically. The difference between these two sorts of curve is that which distinguishes the curve of a bent steel rod from a curve of lead. We search in vain the "Guide" of Hepplewhite and the "Drawing Book" of Sheraton for a suggestion of the characteristic line which is found in practically every chair back of Phyfe's best periods. In them the line of the back posts and the back legs does not form the same continuous, unbroken curve. For this treatment we turn to France, and in the chairs executed during the Directory and early Consulate we have not only this treatment of the back posts and legs but also the methods suggested for many details of decoration. Among the chairs executed by Jacob Frères, 78 rue Meslée, Paris, between 1797 and 1803, are several which contain the germ both of Phyfe's chair design and of his decorative methods. Although it is unlikely that Phyfe actually ever saw a Jacob chair (though some of this furniture may well have been brought to New York) he certainly shared with them the models and published designs from which each developed his style.

That Phyfe correctly interpreted the artistic spirit of his time is shown by this handling of proportion and line. The whole artistic expression of the age tended toward delicacy, refinement, and attenuation. Not only in the proportions of the furniture, but in those of the architecture of the day as well, the tall, slim, vertical element was employed. The classic orders were attenuated, the columns stretched out, the entablatures lightened. Even in women's dress this tendency is seen—the long, high-waisted skirt surmounted by a tiny bodice. This attenuation was indeed a response to some unspoken demand of the time, one of those details which only the psychology of taste may explain, if it can.

The decorative methods and motives of Phyfe's design form the second important element by which his work is distinguished. The methods of decoration include carving, turning, veneering, reeding, and inlay. There is, too, a very occasional use of brass in his best work, although this is much more characteristic of his later periods. The carefully chosen woods which he used, either in solid planks or in veneers, were decorative elements in themselves.

Carving is the most intrinsically fine decorative method found in this, as in every other, furniture. The treatment of the various motives is characteristic and is quite consistent in the different places where it occurs. It is thus a good guide, and for this reason we shall consider all of the carved decoration which is found on Phyfe's furniture of his good periods.

While there is no order of precedence in the consideration of these carved decorative motives, it is best to examine first that decoration which is applied to the supporting structural members such as chair, table, and sofa legs, and pedestals of stands and tables. These may best be arranged in the form of a descriptive list.

ACANTHUS. The most generally used decorative detail in Phyfe work. Found on the upper side of curved legs of pedestal tables, the urn-shaped members of turned pedestals and bed-posts, the fronts of chair legs, the column and post supports of tables, the outer edges of the legs of benches, and in one case on the tall legs of a console table. It is also used on the lyres of pedestal tables and chair backs, tables, sofas, and piano trestles. The acanthus is combined in all of these members with various other details. The most usual combination shows delicate reeding appearing from under the acanthus leaf and completing the decoration of the member. In the round posts and urns the vertical acanthus leaves completely surround the circumference and are superimposed over a plain leaf. The leaf seldom occurs in panels but usually projects beyond the main surface of the wood. The carver's technique employed by Phyfe is consistent. The leaf differs from the acanthus employed in classical decoration, which forms the basis of the details shown in the eighteenth-century design books. Phyfe's acanthus is simplified by the wood-carver's technique into a series of rounded grooves and ridges. The depression seems to have been made with one curved carving tool. This is flanked by two very narrow and shallow depressions from which the raised ridge rounds up. The method is not very different from that in the nulling found in Chippendale work. A raised tapering ridge runs up the whole centre of the leaf, simulating the central vein of the natural form.

This acanthus of Phyfe is very different from that found in design books, on Adam furniture or on that of the French earlier eighteenth-century furniture, which are all more closely related to the acanthus of classic architectural derivation. It partakes much more of the Directoire feeling which was no doubt affected by the flatness of the popular water-leaf ornament of Egyptian and Greek suggestion. The drawings in Plates B, C, and D show this typical leaf decoration.

DOG'S FOOT. This occurs, so far as we know, only on the front legs of chairs on benches and on tables. It was not used very frequently. In this motive the dog's foot is realistically modelled and the hair on the leg is suggested by small, irregular, curved grooves. This motive always finishes the leg at the bottom but runs into some more conventional finish at the top. In one console table, the upper three fifths of the legs are carved with acanthus. In the legs of the lyre-back chair it joins into a rectangular portion the face of which is treated with a narrow panel. The significant detail in the modelling of the foot is that the two outside toes are much subordinated to and drawn back from the two middle ones. (Plate D, Fig. 7.)

WATER LEAF. This delicate ornament decorates the tiny urn-shaped member at the base of some of the earlier chair backs or below the small reeded baluster of sofa arms. (Plate A, Fig. 3.)

PLATE XXXIII. SEWING AND WRITING STAND

PLATE XXXIV. DROP-LEAF TABLE

PLATE XXXV. CARD TABLE, URN PEDESTAL

PLATE XXXVI. CARD TABLE WITH FLUTED DRUM

LEAF AND DART. A simplified form of this occurs on the smaller mouldings of sofa arms and bed-posts. (Plate C, Figs. 1, 2, 3.)

PALM LEAF. An adaptation of the Egyptian palm-leafed, bell-shaped capital is the form found on the top of practically all the bed-posts. The leaves, slightly carved, are merely suggested, with little or no modelling. (Plate C, Figs. 1–4.)

LION'S FOOT. The fine brass feet, in the form of lions' paws, which finish most of the table legs, were varied sometimes by carved wood lions' feet, which cannot be considered a wholly successful substitution. In later work, the lion's foot and leg are used. (Plates XXX, and D, Fig. 9.)

LION'S FOOT AND EAGLE'S WING. In Plate XVI is seen a sofa whose legs are composed of the lion's foot combined with the eagle's wing. It was a feature frequently found in later American Empire furniture, but never with such pleasing effect as in the sofa illustrated, where all the other decoration is restricted to reeding and panelling, which enhances the carving of the legs.

ROSETTES. Sometimes rectangular, or octagonal, sometimes circular, the rosettes are conventionalized forms which require no comment. They occur at the crossing of the reeded members of chair backs, on the corner blocks of tables, and on lyres. (Plates B, Fig. 6, and D, Fig. 3.)

ROPE. The rope motive is rarely used. It does occur between mouldings on the upper side of curved table legs and on the outside edges of lyres which have the acanthus on their faces. It is used also on torus mouldings of the bases of table posts. (Plates B, Fig. 6, and D, Fig. 8.)

FLUTING. The fluting is well placed when it is employed

on the edges of the platforms of pedestal tables, the backs of sofas, or the cylindrical drums of turned table pedestals or bed-posts. (Plates A, Fig. 3, and XL.)

Whorled Fluting. This detail occurs on the bulbous member near the base of certain table supports. The flutes are not so sharp as when straight and parallel and the effect is more nearly that of grooving. (Plates XLIII, and D, Fig. 5.)

Lion Mask. Carved in wood, the lion mask is found on table bases, at the crossing of the reversed curves of Empire sofas, and at the corners of one high-post bedstead. In brass it is used in the same position on chairs and sofas, but these brasses were, of course, not made by Phyfe and were probably imported. (Plates XVII and LV.)

This completes the list of carved decoration on the supporting members of the furniture of the good periods. Other carving occurs in panels which are framed either by one or two delicate reed mouldings or by narrow flat banding. The carved panels fall into two groups: the larger ones, which are found on chair and sofa backs; and the smaller ones, which decorate table skirtings. These panel designs may be studied in the plates of details.

Cornucopiæ. Two crossed cornucopiæ, tied by a bowknot of ribbon. From their mouths issue heads of wheat, laurel leaves, and fruit. The cornucopiæ are carved with a spiral banding. (Plates XVII and A, Fig. 4.)

Laurel. Crossed branches of laurel made into a symmetrical design. (Plates XVII and A, Fig. 8.)

Oak Leaves. A slightly conventionalized branch of oak leaves fills the top panel of one of the chairs. (Plates IV and A, Fig. 2.)

Drapery Swags. A double swag of drapery is caught up in the centre by a bow-knot of ribbon and a cord from which two tassels depend. The ends of the drapery are fastened at points and fall in folds. The edge of the drapery has a delicate indication of fringe. (Plates XII and A, Fig. 5.)

Wheat Ears. A group of ten wheat ears and leaves, crossing in the centre, symmetrically arranged and tied by a bow-knot of ribbon whose ends follow the symmetrical arrangement of the ears. (Plates XII and A, Fig. 6.)

Thunderbolts. Five crossed "thunderbolts," arranged symmetrically and tied by a bow-knot of ribbon. (Plate XIV and A, Fig. 7.)

Trumpets. Two small crossed horns or trumpets tied with a bow-knot of ribbon are found in a panel on one piano base.

More limited in subject are the small panels which are found on table skirtings.

Drapery Swags. Reduced adaptations of the double drapery swags of the larger panels occur as a central medallion on the skirt of card tables. Here the whole is compressed into short space, the bow-knot catches the fringed drapery in the centre, and one or two cords and tassels depend from it. (Plate XLV.)

Prince of Wales Feathers. The three feathers, heraldic device of the Prince of Wales, fill the small rectangular panels above the reeded legs of a card table. Only one example of this usage by Phyfe is known. (Plate XIX.)

Leaf Panels. In one example, a dining-table (Plates

XXXIX and D, Fig. 3), a rectangular unmoulded panel on the base is filled by four acanthus leaves and four plain leaves radiating from a centre. (Plate XXXIX.) A similar design, reduced, occurs on the base of the drop-leaf table. (Plate XL.)

There are certain other motives in which carving shares with veneering, turning, or cut-out design in the total decorative effect.

THE LYRE. The lyre is one of Phyfe's most successful motives. It is employed not only in chair backs—ajouré, to use a French expression—but also in sofa arms, in table supports, and as the supports of dressing glasses. For chair backs and sofa arms, the woodwork is very delicate and the carving of acanthus very subtly and plastically modelled. The strings, either four or five in number, are of brass or whalebone. The key which runs through the top is of ebony. In the crossed lyres of pedestal tables the proportions are a trifle heavier, while as end supports of library tables the thickness of the wood lyre frame is materially increased. For variations of the typical lyres see Plate B of the details.

CHAIR SLATS. The best chair slats are those in which an uncarved medallion, oval, rectangular, or eight-sided, is supported on each side by carved scrolls or groups of leaves. (Plate B.) In some of these the little medallion is plain, but veneered with finely grained wood. In others it is a panel surrounded by a narrow, flat border.

REEDED CROSS-BARS. Chairs showing considerable Sheraton influence are those whose backs are filled by delicately reeded cross-bars. Straight diagonal cross-bars

PLATE XXXVII. SIDE TABLE, FOUR-POST PEDESTAL

PLATE XXXVIII. DROP-LEAF TABLE,
FOUR-POST PEDESTAL

are of two types, single-cross and double-cross. A small carved rosette marks the point where the bars meet. There is also a type with curved cross-bars which meet at a carved medallion. The reeding, too, differs and is made up either of three reeds close together, or of two reeds—really half-round fillets—separated by a flat channel. (Plates I and II.)

The TURNING is certainly the best of its kind. The profiles for the turning are as well designed within their limitations as the carving itself and show free adaptations of the usual forms of base mouldings, necking, fillets, urns, and balusters. The best bits of turning *per se* are the typical Phyfe finish at the bottoms of the straight reeded legs. (Plates XIX and A, Figs 1, 3; and D, Fig 1.) On many of these legs the reeding ends some distance from the floor and the turned portion below is very delicately swelled out, then contracted. Here again the Hepplewhite and Sheraton books help us less than does an examination of the work of Jacob Frères. A few of the reeded legs show an entasis, although most of them taper gently on a straight line. The difficulty of doing fine free turning is best proved by a search for good modern turning, a search invariably rewarded.

There are also delicate little turned and moulded buttons, which are glued over the ends of the tenons of chair backs and rails, where they come through the posts and legs, also on sofa arms and on lyres.

REEDING, which partakes more of the qualities of turning and moulding than it does of carving, is found on almost every piece of Phyfe furniture. Its use contributes largely in emphasizing the slenderness of vertical elements and the delicacy of horizontal. Not only on wood but on marble table-tops do we find this reeding.

VENEERING. Certain uses of veneered decoration may be considered as typical earmarks of Phyfe work. On the rectangular corner blocks which occur on many drop-leaf tables (Plates XX and XXI), the surface is veneered by a small decorative treatment. In some cases it is simply a rectangle of brilliantly grained wood surrounded by a narrow border of the wood contrasting in tone or in the direction of the grain. This rectangle is varied occasionally in two ways. In one, the upper edge of the rectangle breaks out into a semicircle, giving what we call the arched rectangle. (Plate LII.) In other cases the corners of the rectangle are cut off by quarter circles struck with the corner of the rectangle as the centre of the arc. (Plate XXI.) This beautiful treatment, so unobtrusive as to escape notice except upon close examination, is an example of how far the love of his work carried Phyfe in the perfection of craftsmanship. Only a craftsman whose affection for his work far exceeded any desire for gain or showiness could have spent the time and energy on a detail so comparatively insignificant.

These, then, were the design and decorative motives which were comprised in Phyfe's working glossary. In using them he freely changed their size and scale to adapt them correctly to the problems in hand. His combination of forms, his choice of decorative method, and his placing of ornament are all very carefully studied to produce the distinctive quality which appealed to his taste, influenced as it was by the taste of his time. His fondness for beautifully grained woods led him to emphasize this quality of his material by the treatment of veneer and by the reservation of many broad, uncarved surfaces juxtaposed to relief ornaments in panels. His carving, much of it plastic in execution, is always low in relief and avoids any disturbance of the general lines.

As much as any other factor, it is the use of certain decorative forms which gives to all the furniture of Phyfe's best period its unusual consistency. His style is a transitional one, judged by most of his work, and seldom do we find such complete harmony in the combination of elements which make up a style in which a changing taste is recorded. The explanation of this harmony lies entirely in the discrimination which chose so carefully from various styles their most desirable motives and which changed and adapted these motives to use with a feeling for scale, for placing of ornament, and for structural unity unusual in cabinet-makers of any period, and particularly so in a period when all the tendencies were pulling away from the cultivation of a discriminating taste.

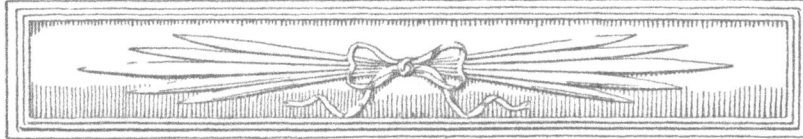

IV

THE FURNITURE

CHAIRS AND BENCHES

CHAIR-MAKING in the eighteenth and early nineteenth centuries was a specialized branch of craftsmanship, distinguished from that of cabinet-making. There were journeyman chair-makers just as there were journeyman cabinet-makers who formed the fluid mass of employed labour upon which the established firms depended. Many of the contemporary newspapers contain advertisements of "fancy" chair-makers who supplied only chairs to their patrons.

Phyfe was both a chair-maker and a cabinet-maker, athough his preference seems to have been for the lighter forms of furniture more closely related in construction to chair-making than they were to heavier cabinet-making. His chief output comprised chairs, tables, and sofas, although in a later chapter will be taken up the miscellaneous articles which he made for special purposes. His chairs are of few types, and the variations of these types are chiefly marked by the decorative elements.

PLATE XXXIX. DINING-TABLE
END VIEW (BELOW) SIDE VIEW (ABOVE)

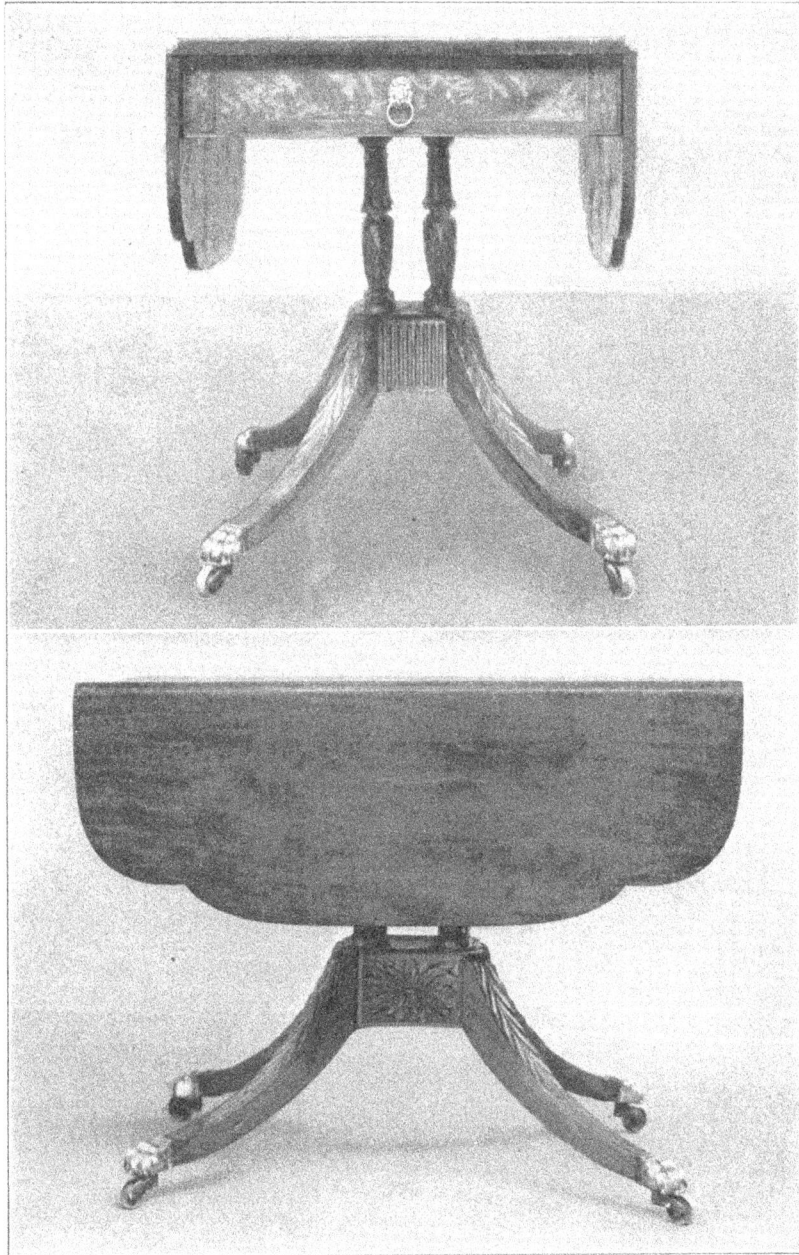

PLATE XL. DROP-LEAF TABLE. END AND
SIDE VIEWS

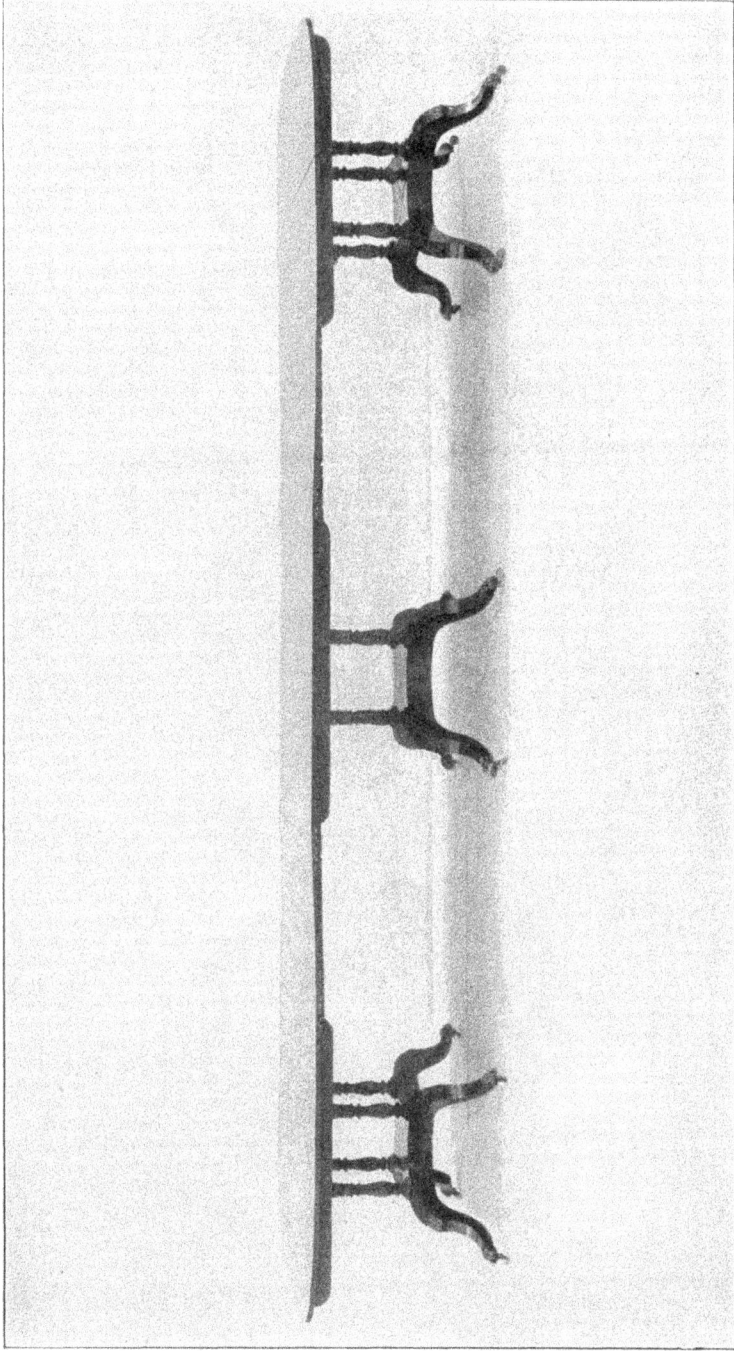

PLATE XLI. EXTENSION DINING-TABLE

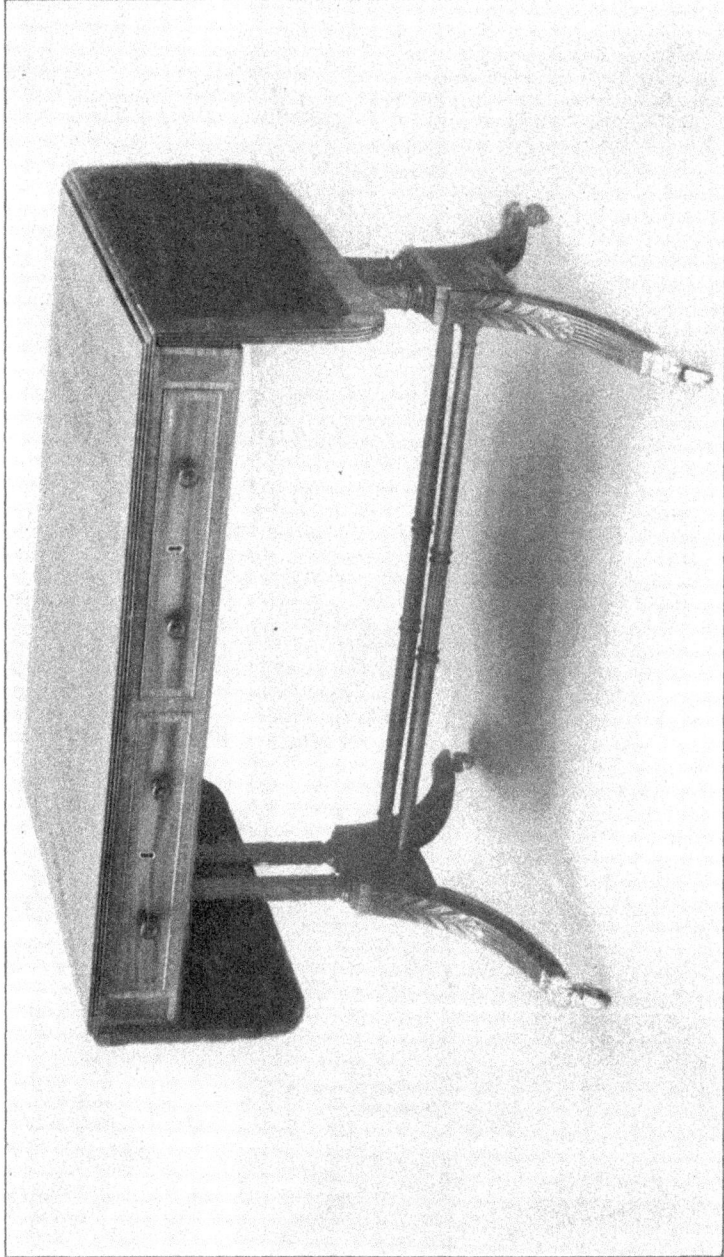

PLATE XLII. SOFA TABLE WITH END SUPPORTS

The type of chair which is earliest in style, if not in point of date, is that in which the Sheraton influence is strongest. This type has the horseshoe-shaped seat, with two straight reeded legs in front and with back legs gently curved, continuing the line of the back posts.

In this type, the known variations are as follows: The horseshoe seat is reeded as are the back posts, the crossbars of the back, and the front legs which terminate in small brass lions' feet below the characteristic baluster turning at the bottom. The two diagonal crossbars are reeded and an oval rosette marks the crossing. The upper back panel is carved with the "thunderbolt" or wheat design. (Plate I.) A second variation has a double-crossing of four reeded diagonal bars with two rosettes. (Plate II.) A third variation differing slightly from the others retains the horseshoe seat with reeded edge and the same curves of the back posts and top panel. It is distinguished by the employment of curved bars in the back edged by half-round fillets and joined by a small eight-sided rosette. Its legs, rectangular in plan and set at a 45° angle, are gentle reverse curves with the fronts carved in acanthus. They end in brass lions' feet. The carved top panel of the back has the laurel pattern. (Plate II.)

The full Directoire influence is seen in the easy, flowing lines of the second type of chair. The decorative elements which are combined in this are the lyre, the dog's foot, the carved slat, the acanthus, reeding, and plain panels. There are numerous combinations which were made—the lyre back with dog's foot or acanthus legs, the carved slat back with both of these legs, and both of these backs with moulded front legs. The curve of the back posts is not continuous, breaking slightly at the junction of the seat rails with the line flowing more definitely into the seat than into the back legs. The front of the back posts and upper side of the side seat rails are reeded, the front seat rail is reeded below the loose, upholstered seat. The top panel of the back is uncarved but veneered with elaborately grained wood, although one example has this member fluted. The front legs are cut in a gentle concave curve. The lyres and carved slats are of the type described in the preceding chapter. Small turned buttons cover the ends of the tenons of the front seat rail and the top panel of the back.

A third general type of chair exhibits the introduction of Empire influence in the legs which are composed of double reverse curves, crossed in the centre, plain or reeded, and ending in brass lions' feet. Of this type two arrangements of legs occur, one with the curved legs on both sides joined with a turned stretcher, the other with the curved legs at the front and the usual square legs at the back. (Plate XIII.) In the latter the stretcher from the crossing of the curves runs back to join a stretcher between the two back legs. The top back panel in chairs of this type is usually carved with laurel. The meeting of the intersecting curves of the legs is marked by either a turned button or a lion's mask. The backs of the type are filled with either curved or diagonal bars.

These are the three general types of chair from point of view of form. A few exceptions occur, however, which are simply different combinations of elements included among those already mentioned. An armchair of each of these three types is illustrated. The first, with reverse-curved

acanthus legs, reeded horseshoe seat, curved back bars
and laurel panel, matches a similar side chair. (Plate III.)
The second, with concave moulded legs, reeded arms and
back posts, has an eight-sided panel in the centre of the slat
supported by carved scrolls. The panel is surrounded by
a flat raised band. The material is curly mahogany. (Plate
B, Fig. 8.) The third armchair has the crossed reverse
curves at the side joined by a turned stretcher. It has
curved back bars and laurel panel at top. The illustration
of this chair shows also a footstool made as part of the same
drawing-room set from which the chair comes. (Plate XI.)

The arms of the first and third types are curved and rest
upon turned balusters, in one case reeded. It is the same arrangement as the Phyfe sofa arm and is Sheraton in derivation. The arm of the second type of chair is set on a scroll.

In all of these chairs the top line of the back dips down in
a curve which adds to comfort as well as beauty, while the
decoration is combined in many ways and undoubtedly
was used in other combinations in chairs which have not
come down to us.

The little window benches are more closely related to
chairs than they are to sofas. The arms are simply reduced
replicas, in line and detail, of the chair backs. The hand-
somest one is that with the laurel-leaf pattern in the top
panel above the curved bars. The little urn-form at the
base of the posts is carved with water-leaf ornament and
the legs, ending in brass lions' feet, are enriched by the
acanthus. A second bench has no carving except the
small rosette at the crossing of the back bars, while a
third has the upper panel fluted to match the chairs of

the same set.   One very fine bench rests upon the dog feet, its rails are carved into panels of drapery, and its seat and arms are upholstered.

A number of chairs, similar in form to the second type which we have described, were made in New York with a slat entirely carved with cornucopiæ or fruit and flowers. So far as we know, Phyfe did not make any chairs of this sort, at least in his best period.   The distinguishing marks of the Phyfe chairs are their lines and proportion; the presence of reeding (in his later chairs reeding was at times replaced by moulding); the gentle sag of the top of the back; the outward splay of the side rails which are never parallel; and lastly the decoration by carving, reeding, moulding, panelling, or turning, in his accustomed designs.

The material is always mahogany, in some cases curly mahogany.   The strings of the lyre are brass or whalebone, the key handles and tips of ebony.   The seats are either loose, upholstered ones held in place by screws, or they are caned.   The latter were covered by loose, squab cushions.

These, then, are the three main types of chairs with their variations which the illustrations will present more clearly than any verbal description.

PLATE XLIII. LIBRARY TABLE

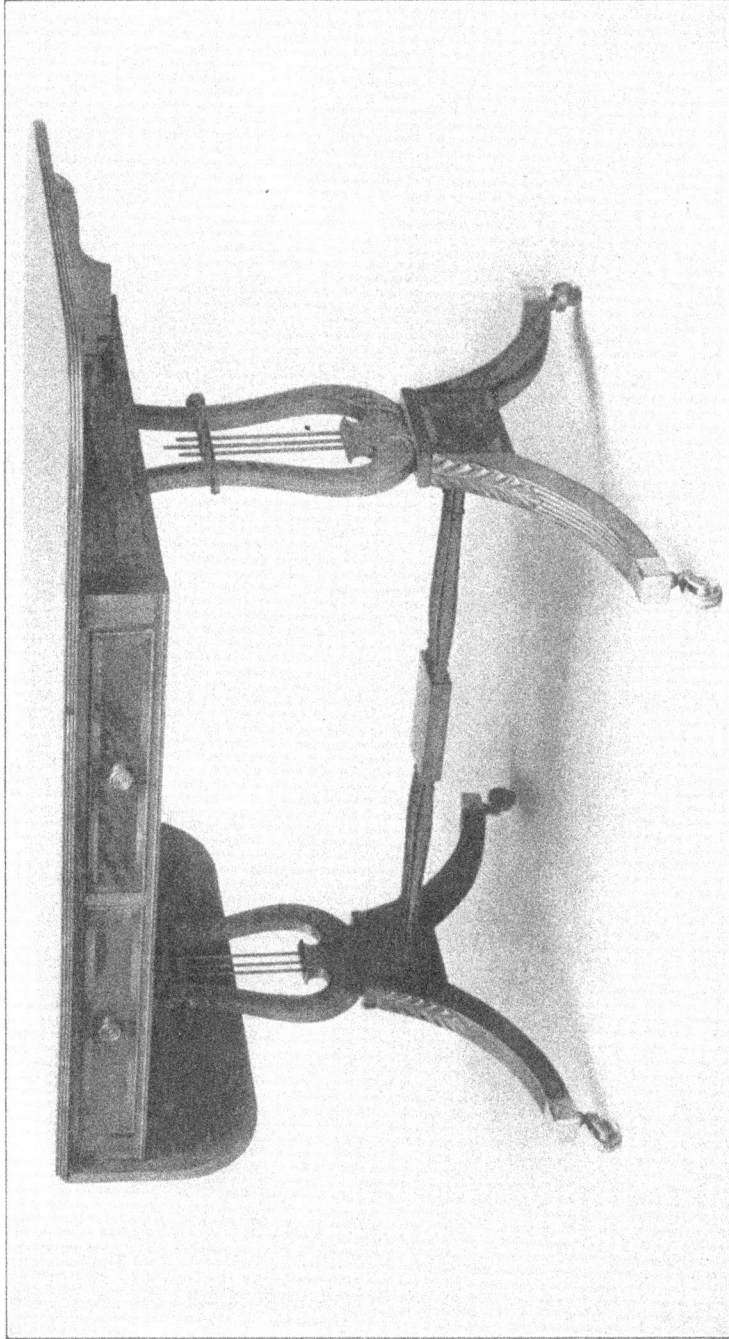

PLATE XLIV. SOFA TABLE

PLATE XLV. CARD TABLE, CROSSED LYRE PEDESTAL

PLATE XLVI. CARD TABLE, CROSSED LYRE
PEDESTAL

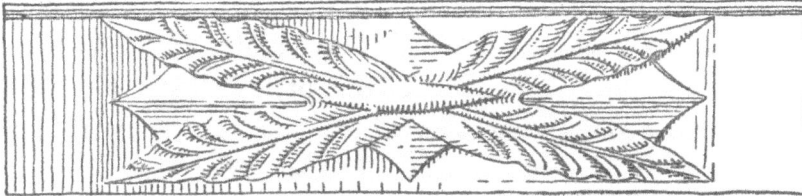

V

THE FURNITURE

SOFAS

THE sofas are closely related to the chairs, which they frequently were made to match—that is to say, certain of the forms or carved decorations found in the chairs are repeated in the sofas. In the sofas we have practically the same three types seen in the chairs, although in this case they are not so definitely demarked one from another.

The first and most usual type is Sheraton of a form much used both in America and in England at the end of the eighteenth century. This is the design with a straight wooden top rail decorated in some way, wooden curved arms resting on small balusters, wooden front and side rails straight or partly curved, and six or eight legs, always four in front. (Plates XII and XIV.)

In the Phyfe sofas of this group the top rail of the back is panelled, usually into three rectangular panels. These panels are carved with typical ornament—drapery swags, "thunderbolts," wheat, or fluting—and are surrounded with one or two half-round fillet mouldings. The top edges of the arms which continue the curve of the back are reeded and end in a slight scroll which turns under and rests upon a small baluster. The shaft of this little baluster is reeded and the urn-shaped member at its base carved with leaf ornament. The arms in most of these sofas curve slightly out, then in, which gives them an inviting air. Some, however, come straight forward at right angles to the back.

The front and side rails of the seat, which form a continuous frame, are reeded. In the straight-armed sofas, the front rail of the seat is straight and covered by the upholstery; in those with curved arms, the front rail of the seat is reeded, not covered by upholstery, and joins the side rail on a wide curve, on which the baluster of the arm is set at an angle. The short legs, too, are reeded and are usually turned to a profile with a slight entasis. The bottom member of the leg is the slightly bulging turning.

These sofas are upholstered, arms, back, and seat, or are caned. The main variations of this type are those resulting from combinations of ornament in the back panels. There are examples of all of these variations, where the front seat rail is covered with upholstery.

Unlike chairs of the second type, that showing Directoire influence, the sofas of this second group are few and far between. The most striking example is that with twin lyres in the arms shown in Plate XV. Here are seen several innovations. The top is of figured mahogany in one long narrow panel. From the back a short but finely sweeping curve runs out and joins that of the arms. The arms in profile resemble the lyre-back chair, with plain top panel and the two lyres, side by side, ajouré, fill the space below. The lines of the arms sweep down into that of the seat rail. The legs are made up of scrolls in cornucopia form. Reeding preponderates in the decoration, though a little fine carving occurs on the lyres. The back and seat are upholstered.

Much the same lines of seat, arms, and back occur in the sofa in Plate XVI. Here three plain panels fill the top rail, while arms, seat, and back are upholstered. In the legs, however, is seen a decided Empire touch, made up as they are of lion's foot and eagle's wing. This is one of the most graceful and distinguished of Phyfe sofas.

We know of no sofas or settees carrying out literally the lines of the chairs of the second type. They may not have seemed desirable for practical reasons, since the concave legs on the chairs, if repeated in the centre of a sofa, would project in front of the seat rail and interfere with comfortable use. These other two solutions are much better studied than such a chair-back settee would have been.

The third type, Empire in character, is represented by two treatments of the same scheme. In the splendid drawing-room suite from which our cane-seated Empire chair comes is the handsome sofa shown in Plate XVII. In this, the upper portion reflects the general Directoire lines of the preceding two sofas, but the legs are treated with the crossed reverse curves, brass lions' heads at their crossing and brass lions' feet at their base. The legs and arms are reeded and the back and arm panels are carved with laurel branches and with crossed cornucopiæ. The back, arms, and seat are caned and loose cushions were tied over them. The proportions and general lines are very fine, the only point which can be criticized being the junction between the curved legs and the front rail. This remarkable sofa is still in the possession of the family for which it was made and is part of a suite comprising also side chairs, armchairs, footstools, and console tables. The little settee shown in Plate XXIII is a single treatment of the crossed curved legs whose proportions are rendered heavier for support. The carved panels of the back, contracted into different proportions from those usually found, are all from designs found in the sofas of the first type. The reeded seat rails of this and the preceding piece are straight.

These sofas show the approach of the chair-maker to the more ambitious problem and indicate clearly how much more than a chair-maker Phyfe was. The relationship which they bear to the chairs is proper, but the new problem is met on its own ground and advantage taken of all its possibilities. In construction great care is shown, the seat supports underneath the caning are gently curved to allow for the elasticity of the cane, and these supports are mortised into a dove-tailed groove in the seat rail, a refinement of construction which renders easily distinguishable Phyfe's work from good reproduction.

From these sofas and chairs we may be able to draw some conclusions as to their chronology. In those of the Sheraton type the carved panel details are the drapery swags, thunderbolts, wheat ears, and fluting. In the most characteristic Empire chairs and sofas we find the laurel used practically always, combined with cornucopiæ panels. These latter details probably succeed the War of 1812 when patriotic

PLATE XLVII. SIDEBOARD WITH VENEERED,
CARVED, AND REEDED DECORATIONS

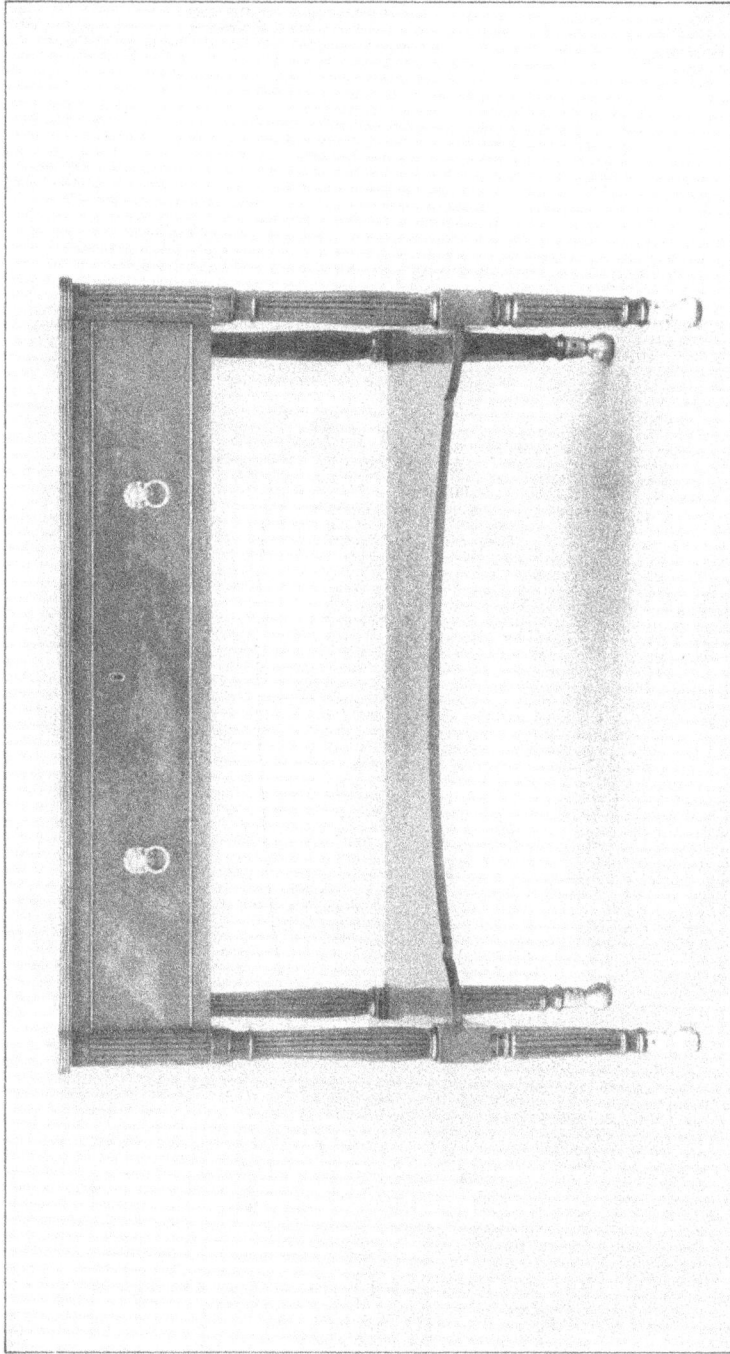

PLATE XLVIII. SERVING TABLE

PLATE XLIX. BUFFET

PLATE L. SERVING TABLE

motives were much in vogue. Of French origin, these motives were coming over at about this time and with the prosperous years succeeding the war these two decorative motives, one symbolic of glory or victory, the other symbolizing
plenty and fruitfulness, the results of successful war, were
popular. We know that one of the suites comprising these
details was made about 1817.

The decorative details of the Sheraton sofas would bespeak
a date between 1800 and 1813, when combined with purely
Sheraton form. However, their employment on the small
Empire sofa (Plate XVIII) would suggest that Phyfe felt
their quality so lasting as not to be affected by fads or styles,
and he has retained them here. We may conclude that it
is impossible to date Phyfe furniture exactly from the
decorative elements alone, but only from a combination of the
furniture form and decoration. And even this method is
not wholly satisfactory, for we know that some of the simple
Sheraton Pembroke tables were made as late as 1820. It
is well, therefore, not to be too meticulous in dating the
furniture of his good periods, but rather to relate its changes
purely stylistically, and date it all between 1800 and 1825,
although that with Empire features may be placed after
1813.

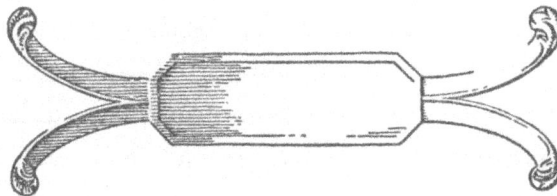

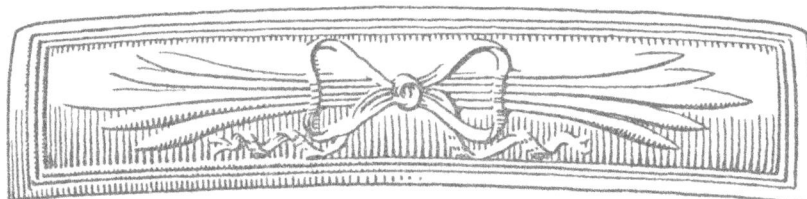

VI

THE FURNITURE

TABLES

THE number and variety of Phyfe's tables are so great as to render very difficult their classification into groups from which there shall not be a number of exceptions. The uses for which these tables were made are many. There are card, console, and library tables, dining, serving, and sofa tables, sewing, dressing, writing tables, and candle-stands.

In general structural form, they fall into one of three types: the first, with legs at the corners; the second, supported upon a pedestal of one sort or another; the third, supported at the ends. They differ very much in the shape of the tops, in the treatment of the supporting elements of legs and pedestals, as well as in the inclusion of drawers.

The first type, the earliest stylistically though not necessarily chronologically, is supported on straight reeded legs. It includes the fine Sheraton card tables such as those illustrated in Plates XIX and XX, the Pembroke table with reeded legs (Plate XXII), the dining-tables such as that in Plate XXIII, and the game table (Plate XXI). Here we have simple, straightforward table construction, carefully studied for stability and use, the proportions beautifully balanced and the decoration suppressed. The legs are generally reeded and end in the typical turned member at the bottom. The skirtings are veneered and have a narrow border whose grain runs in a different direction from that of the rest of the wood. The corner blocks are either veneered or carved with small panel decoration. The tops are often shaped in the cloverleaf pattern and the edges of the tops are not often reeded.

The significant points for attribution are the construction details, the typical carved or veneered ornament, the turned member at the bottom of the reeded legs, and the subtle curve in the clover-leaf top.

The three finest tables in the type are the game table in Plate XXI and the card tables in Plates XX and XIX. The game table exhibits not only ingenuity in its arrangement, but great beauty of line and proportion. The removable top, baize-covered on one side, hides a backgammon board sunk below the surface. The points are inlaid in ivory, alternating white and green, and little ivory sockets around the edge receive the scoring pegs. A small drawer at the right of each player is for the counters. Below the central portion of the skirting, between the drawer fronts, is concealed a chess board which slides out and is placed over the backgammon board, whose space it fits exactly, lying flush with the top. Nothing could be simpler, nothing more perfectly adapted to use. The corner blocks are veneered with the small rectangle with concave corners.

The two card tables are purely Sheraton, the one with light mahogany veneer on the skirt enhanced by veneered blocks, the other with carved central and corner blocks, the latter with the Prince of Wales feathers. The clover-leaf tops show the subtle curve mentioned as a Phyfe characteristic.

The Pembroke tables, such as that in Plate XXII, contain one drawer whose front is edged by a half-round fillet. The corner blocks are veneered.

The fine dining table (Plate XXIII), is enriched only by a narrow banding of dark wood at the bottom of the skirt, this banding running across the blocks above the legs in place of a veneered rectangle.

A variation of this four-legged type of table is seen in a pair of flap-leaf console tables whose corners are cut off at a 45° angle, the legs set at this angle and composed of a reverse curve decorated with acanthus joining with the dog's leg and foot. Medallions above are carved with rosettes, while the central block has a panel of carved drapery swags. The edge is not reeded.

The second type, the pedestal table, has two main divisions. In one of these the pedestal is composed of a turned central support from which curving legs spread out. In the second there is a platform which the curving legs support, and upon this platform rests the portion upholding the superstructure of the table.

Within the first group of this type the turned support is designed in several forms, the most usual of which has a

PLATE LI. CHEVAL GLASS

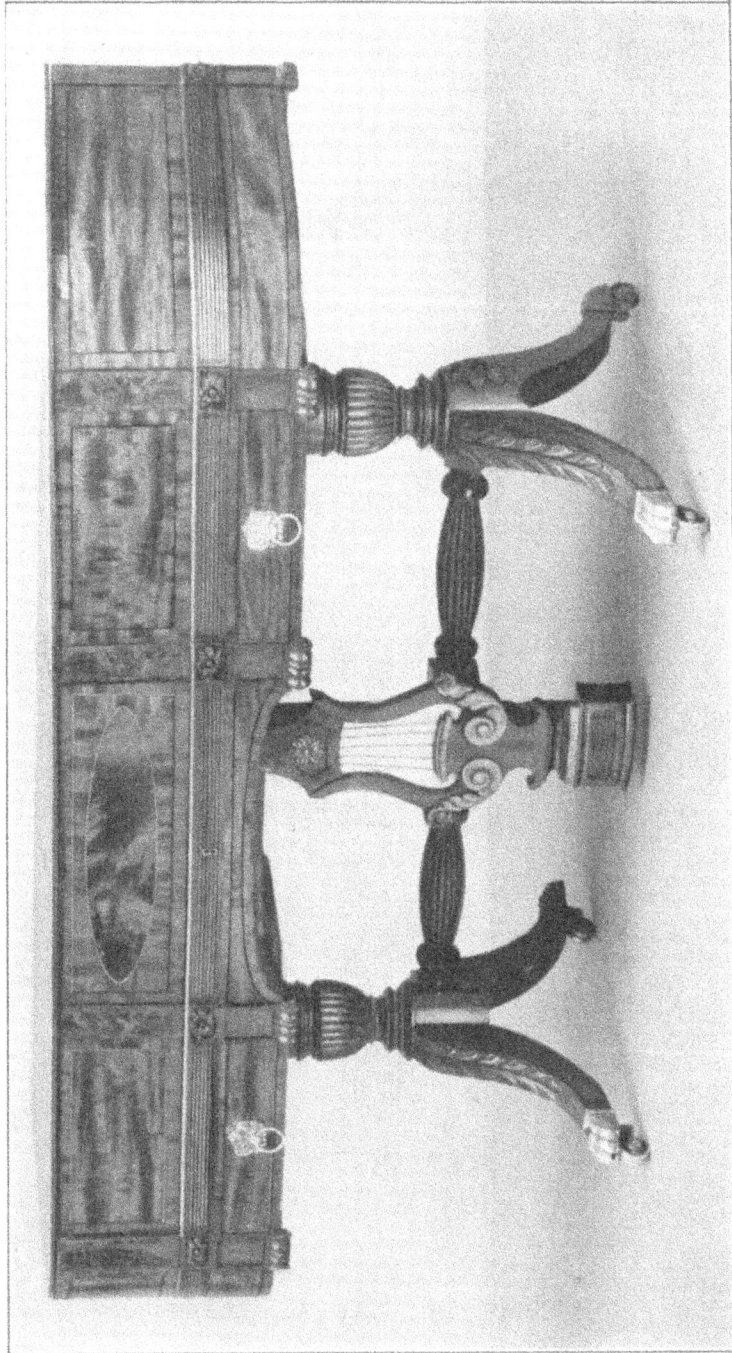

PLATE LII. PIANO CASE AND TRESTLE

large urn-shaped member as its predominating feature.
The urn is sometimes plain, more often carved with acanthus
or reeded. The base moulding about the urn is frequently
carved. Another of these turned shafts (Plate XXXVI) is
undecorated except for a broad reeded drum near its base.
The legs—three or four—are either carved with acanthus
and reeding on their top surfaces or are moulded. The
feet are lion's paws, usually brass, although sometimes of
wood. The tables with this form of base include drop-leaf
tables and those card tables with three legs, with or without
skirting, containing a mechanism by which, when the flap
is lowered, the rear leg swings out and forms with the other
two an accurate tripod (Plate XXXII). The small sewing
stands with rounded ends are often supported on this type
of base, while the little tripod stand with tip-top (Plate
XXVIII) is a rare example in the type.

The tops are curved in single curve or clover-leaf pattern.
A border of veneer usually surrounds them. The edges are
sometimes reeded, the skirtings veneered, and in the drop-
leaf tables the corner blocks—relict of the straight-leg
Pembroke—are veneered in designs and finished with a
delicate turned drop. These tables are among Phyfe's most
characteristic product. This type includes card and console, sewing, writing, and dining tables, such as those illustrated in Plates XXXIII and XXXV.

In the second group of the pedestal tables, a platform
upon which vertical supports rest is upheld by curved legs.
This group must be subdivided into two kinds. The first
division comprises those tables whose super-structure is
supported upon four posts which rest upon the little plat-

form. The second division includes the tables in which crossed lyres act as the immediate support of the portion above.

Of the type with four posts, the chief variations result from differently turned balusters which follow several forms, such as those shown in the drawings in Plate E. The sides of the platforms are either plain, panelled, fluted, or carved with a rectangular rosette made up of acanthus and plain leaves radiating from a centre. These tables are illustrated in Plates XXXIII to XLI, and include sewing and writing stands, drop-leaf centre tables, side tables with a flap, and dining tables.

The lyre-base tables have few varieties. The one in Plate XLVI has the rope motive on the tops of the curved legs and on the edges of the lyre. The second one, in Plate XLV, would appear to be from Phyfe's later period. The lion's feet and legs are a trifle clumsy, while the overloading with acanthus deprives the lyre of much of its delicacy. This table resembles in so many ways the work of a certain Philadelphian contemporary of Phyfe that its inclusion would be confusing without definitely mentioning it as a late piece whose attribution is chiefly based upon structural details not part of its stylistic quality.

The last general type of table, that whose supports are at the end, includes library, sofa, and dressing tables. The type is rare, but excellent as a new solution of the problem.

In Plate XLIII is shown a library table, supported on coupled colonettes at each end, from whose fluted base-block spread out two legs. The top contains a drawer, while a shelf for books is placed below. This is a good

PLATE LIII. HIGH-POST BEDSTEAD

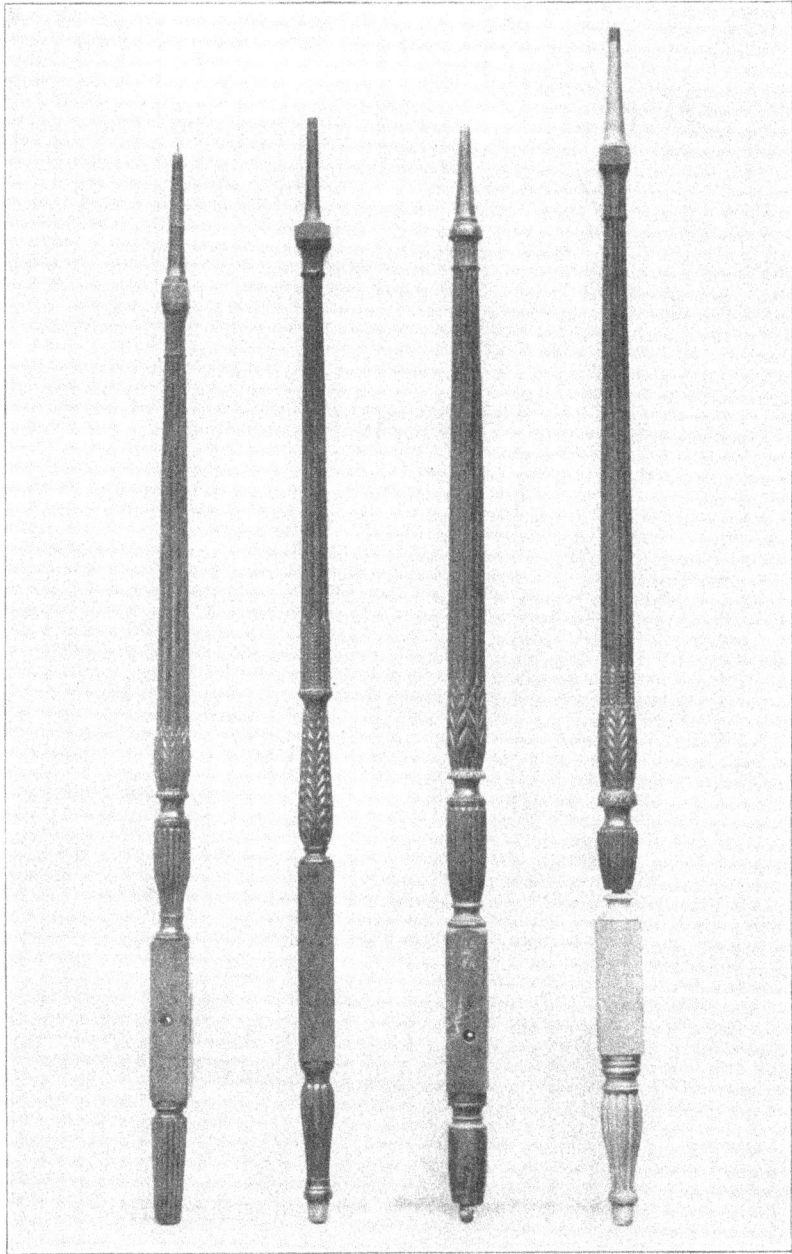

PLATE LIV. FOUR TYPES OF BEDPOSTS

example of variation of proportion in studying a special problem. The thickness of the skirting, controlled by the depth of the drawer, is related pleasantly to the whole height of the piece. The decoration exhibits the typical methods and designs. The whorled carving and the acanthus leaves on the colonettes are similar to those in the pair of side tables, one of which is shown in Plate XXXVII.

Very similar to this is a man's dressing table not illustrated. Here the interior is fitted with a mirror and with compartments necessary for toilet articles and accessories. All of the interior cabinet work is beautifully done, the edges of the compartments reeded, and little boxes fitted into the divisions.

Two sofa tables (Plates XLII and XLIV) are superb examples of absolutely finished workmanship. The ends of one are supported upon a lyre, the ends of the other on coupled colonettes. The stretchers in both are beautiful and delicate; the veneering on the drawers and around the top is brilliantly contrasting; the edges are reeded and the drop leaves curved. These are both exceptional pieces. The lyre is much heavier than those in chairs, sofas, or tables. It is carved with acanthus and its edges are reeded.

These three types of table include a great number of variations both in design and decoration. They introduce many decorative motives unlike those on the sofas.

In all of these we see the careful finish of the construction which would ordinarily not be found in furniture of the period, and the introduction of the tiny details in veneered designs which are seen only upon careful examination. This careful finish bespeaks more than the qualities of a good workman; it marks the work of an artist-craftsman whose interest and love were in his work, and whose completely rounded training included both broad design and minute detail with complete technical adequacy.

VII

THE FURNITURE

MISCELLANEOUS PIECES

THE large number of miscellaneous pieces bearing the mark of Phyfe's handiwork belies the statement that he did not do case furniture. Certainly he did many pieces of so-called case furniture, but these were probably made on special order to go into rooms where his tables, chairs, or sofas had delighted their owners with their beauty and their livable qualities.

One of the most interesting problems which Phyfe had to meet occasionally was that of the pianoforte. Very few of these survive. The one illustrated herewith (Plate LII), dating from about 1820, contains an instrument by John Geib, Inc., whose work in New York began before 1800 and continued until after 1825. Phyfe is supposed not to have made piano cases, but only the trestles which supported the cases. This case, however, bears so many unmistakable signs of Phyfe's handiwork as to leave little doubt that he made both case and trestle. The case is veneered in brilliantly grained wood, is inlaid with brass, and the vertical blocks, which divide the front into three

79

sections, are veneered with the typical arched rectangle. Reeding, too, is used, and carved rosettes. The composition of the front of the case is well studied. It is divided into three sections, the two to the left lifting up and disclosing the keyboard.

The trestle is designed on a basis of Phyfe's typical motives—the urn, the curved legs with acanthus and reeding, the reeded stretcher, and at the end a carved flower instead of the more probable lion's head. A lyre in the centre suggests the original presence of pedals, but it would appear upon examination that pedals never existed. The strings of the instrument are covered by a thin, hinged wooden lid painted green with a flower border.

Another piano trestle (Plate LV) differs in detail from the first. The urns here are carved with acanthus, the stretcher is not divided into two parts as was the other, and its end, where it mortises into the block below the urn is treated with a lion's mask. Its proportions, too, are lighter, since it probably supported a smaller case without pedals.

The little sideboard (Plate XLVII) and the serving tables in Plates XLVII to L are consistently Sheraton in derivation. The sideboard is a most surprising find— a complete piece of Phyfe case furniture handled in masterly fashion. Here veneering forms the chief decoration including arched rectangles with borders mitred up to them, veneered borders on the drawers and around the top, the edge bounded by two half-round fillets and a flat channel, the reeded legs topped by acanthus leaves and finished at the bottom with the typical turning. Surely a fine, simple, dignified little sideboard, worthy descendant of Sheraton's design.

The serving table and buffet are Sheraton, too, but of simpler forms and less elaborate decoration. The legs are reeded and carry up to the top, which curves out over them at the corners. They preserve the same simplicity as do the tables of the first type.

The cheval glass (Plate LI) makes us wonder why Phyfe did so few of these graceful articles of bedroom furniture. He did dressing-table glasses of the same general character although more carefully decorated. One dressing glass is swung between lyres turned at right angles to its axis and rests upon a base with three drawers. The edges of the lyres are roped, the base between the drawers decorated with little turned colonettes.

His beds were derived both from Sheraton and Hepplewhite models. The one shown in Plate LII has four carved posts, although some of them have only the two footposts carved, the headposts being simply turned pieces. There are seven different known designs for bedposts, four of which are shown in Plate C of the drawings. The decoration includes reeding, acanthus, water-leaf, drapery, wheat-ears, and palmetto, combined in various charming ways. One handsome bed, not shown, has a footboard filled with cane and with lions' masks at the corners of the heavy posts.

VIII

CONCLUSION

Much discussion in recent years has centred around the "humanities," the related study and cultivation of the languages, literature, history, and archæology of Greece and Rome. It is the conviction of their value as a moral or intellectual discipline and as refining, cultivating, and humanizing influences which has led their supporters to include the "humanities" as a necessary part of a liberal education. The resultant knowledge which such studies give creates a background for modern life and a sense of values that are difficult if not impossible of attainment in any other way.

As a part of a liberal education to-day, the scope of the so-called "humanities" has necessarily widened beyond the original limits, and in the new sense must include much of the literature, history, and art of epochs of the world's development successive to the times of classic Greece and Rome. This wider application of the term may justly be employed if we think of the "humanities" as an investigation less of things Greek and Roman than of things secular and human.

In humanizing any period of the past, the study not only of the contemporary languages, literature, and history is important, but that of the artistic expression of the time must also be closely related to them. The four major arts do not alone suffice to tell the human story of a time gone by. They indicate frequently the highest aspirations or accomplishments which marked the summit of a people's development. For the more true, more accurate story, filled with human interest and marking a high average of general taste, we must turn to the decorative and utilitarian arts with which that people surrounded themselves in their daily life.

We may learn of the great movements of races, the international give-and-take of territory or riches; we may fill in this knowledge with a just proportion of economic detail and of religious and moral influences; but to round out the picture of a particular people at a particular time we must appreciate the intellectual, artistic, and social elements which entered into their daily life, which influenced them continually and responded to their tastes and preferences, æsthetic and practical.

The study of the finest work of the cabinet-makers of the past thus bears a distinct relation to the general humanizing investigation of any period of world history, and the importance of such study is in direct proportion to the importance of the period in question.

The short space of a quarter of a century in New York which we have striven to portray was certainly one of the most important in the whole history of the city's growth. It was marked by a striking increase in economic prosperity and commercial expansion, a growth of civic consciousness and pride, a vivid interest in artistic and intellectual pursuits, a horizon widening from that of a provincial town to that of a metropolis, with the emphasis upon foreign taste and foreign ways which was a natural accompaniment. The War of 1812 was a quickening influence in the direction of consolidating this civic consciousness, as it was in binding together all parts of the Union. The Constitution had weathered its first real storm and the policies of its creators were justified. The economic revival after the war was rapid, and the city and nation entered upon a fortunate period of peace and prosperity.

In the qualities of the furniture which Duncan Phyfe made for the people of New York at this time may be seen the results of the varied influences which distinguished the period, not only in the city but along the whole seaboard. The demand for fine craftsmanship and materials arose directly from both the increasing wealth of the population and the artistic appreciation which they possessed. The unanimity of taste which resulted from the growth of a compact metropolitan society is reflected in the consistency and restraint of the furniture design which appealed to them, a design whose simplicity recalled in romantic association the glories of an earlier republic, that of Rome. Their widening horizon is shown in the European flavour which permeates much of this work, partially English in response to inherent British preferences, but French in many elements of form where fashion dictated. The intellectual

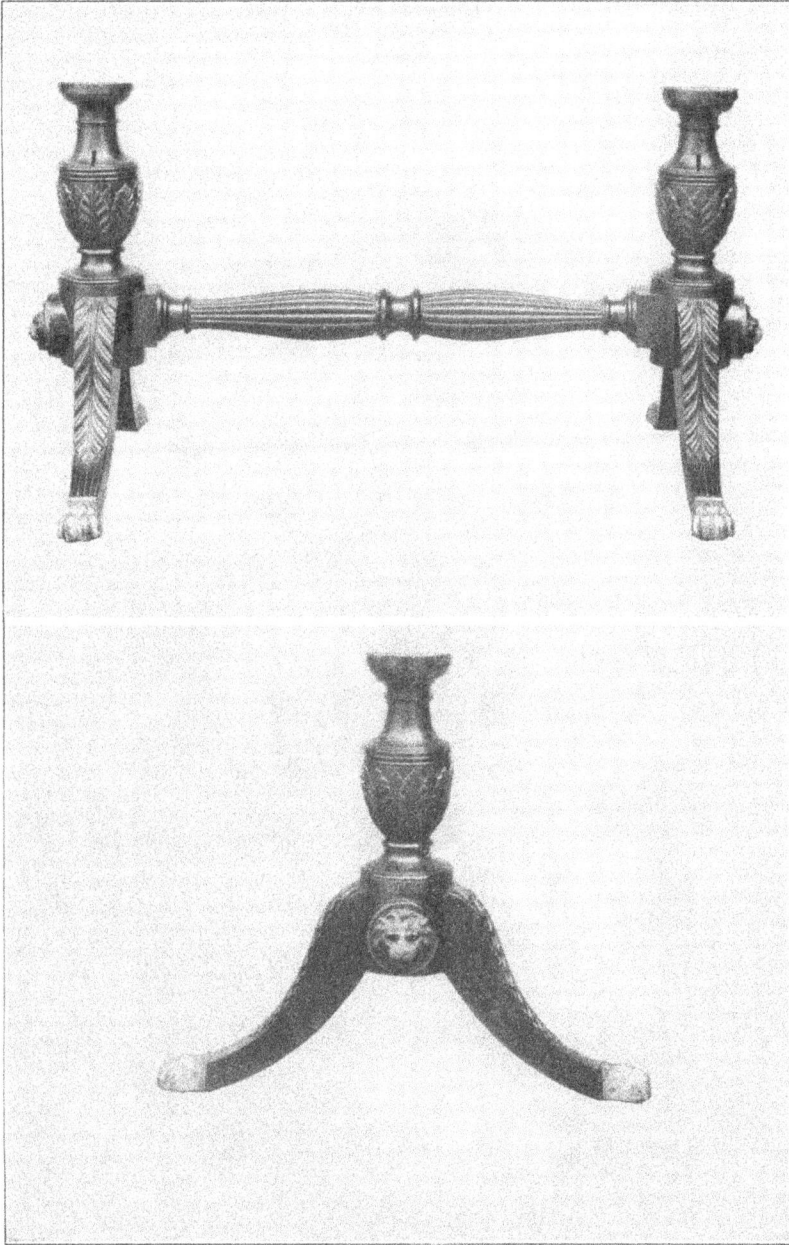

PLATE LV. TRESTLE FOR A PIANO

PLATE LVI. WASHSTAND

content in the design bespeaks distinctly an appreciative taste in those who so fully felt its refinement and delicate subtlety.

Thus in the work of Phyfe we have an apposite example of how closely the utilitarian and decorative arts are bound up with all the other phases of human civilization and progress. His work was a development of an old tradition within the limits of which his own art advanced, responding to many contemporary influences.

This tradition had continued as long as the interest of creative minds was turned in its direction, but with the growth of scientific investigation in the nineteenth century the preponderant interests of the cultivated public and of its creative minds swung away from artistic creation to that of scientific development. It is natural that the great industrial revolution of the nineteenth century should thus have diverted to itself most of the creative energy which for many centuries had given expression in artistic form to a part of its power. Robert Fulton and Samuel F. B. Morse are examples of men whose lives spanned this transition from art to science and whose creative energies could be turned to one or the other for the benefit of either.

There is one idea which should perhaps lead all others in a consideration of the work of Phyfe. That is the importance of the artistic tradition which he carried with him through his best years, a tradition which his furniture expresses as perfectly as does the dignified architecture of the early republic.

This artistic tradition was the heritage of the United States long before their independence was achieved. It still remained their heritage for fifty years afterward, only then to be cast aside. To this tradition it would seem logical to return again if within its limitations can be properly comprised the requirements, utilitarian and æsthetic, which the taste and usage of modern times demand. And for a suggestion of how one skillful furniture-designer and cabinet-maker utilized this tradition and adapted it to his own time, a study of Phyfe's handiwork offers much valuable help and tells a tale of high ideals in workmanship, of beauty, grace, and imagination in design, and of a close approximation to the requirements of usage as dictated by social custom, elements which are the essentials of all utilitarian art which deserves to rank as handmaid to the great art of architecture.

A

1

2

3

4

5

6

7

8

9

ROWLAND

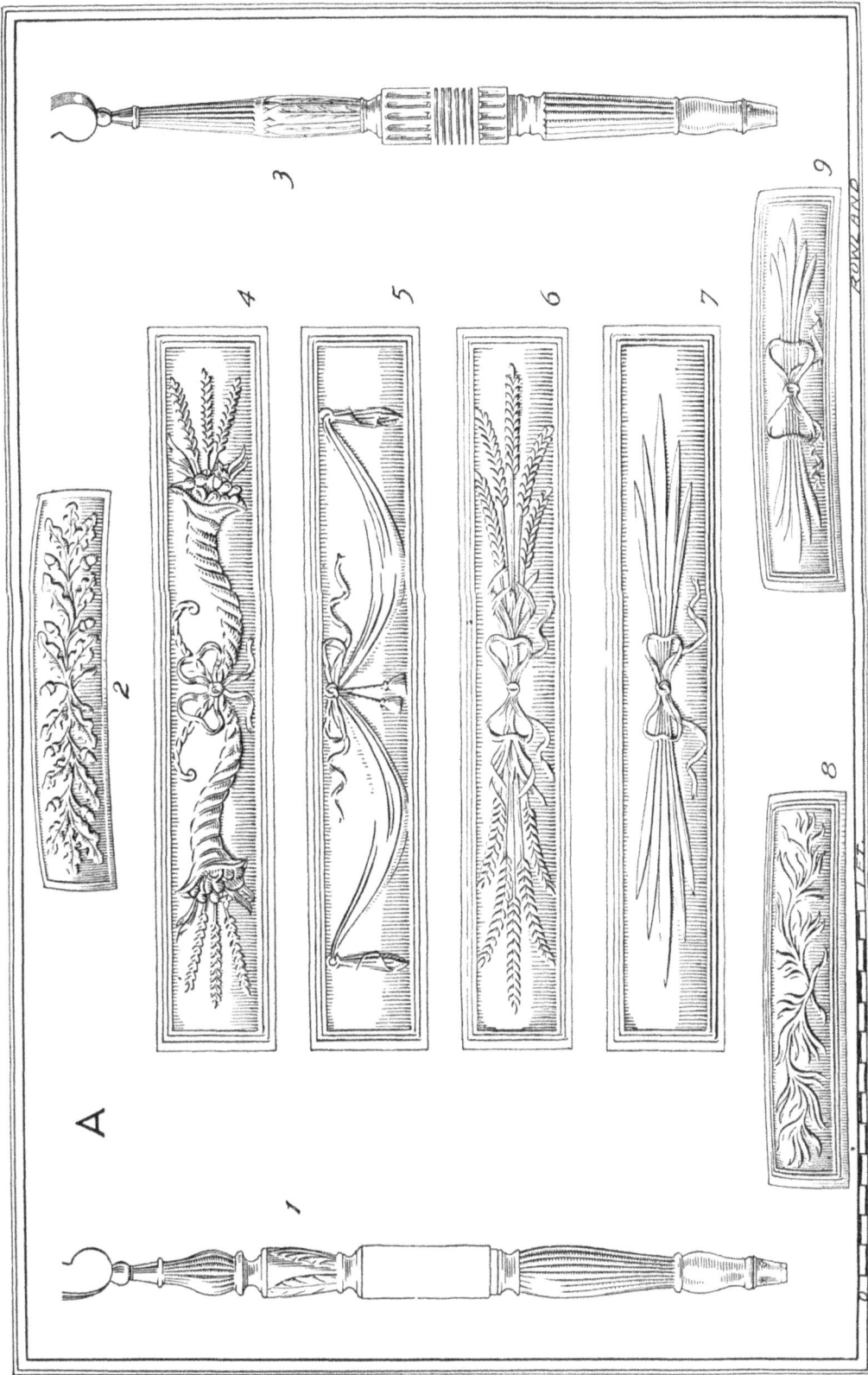

DETAILS OF SOFA ARMS AND LEGS. CARVED PANELS FROM SOFAS AND FROM CHAIR-BACKS

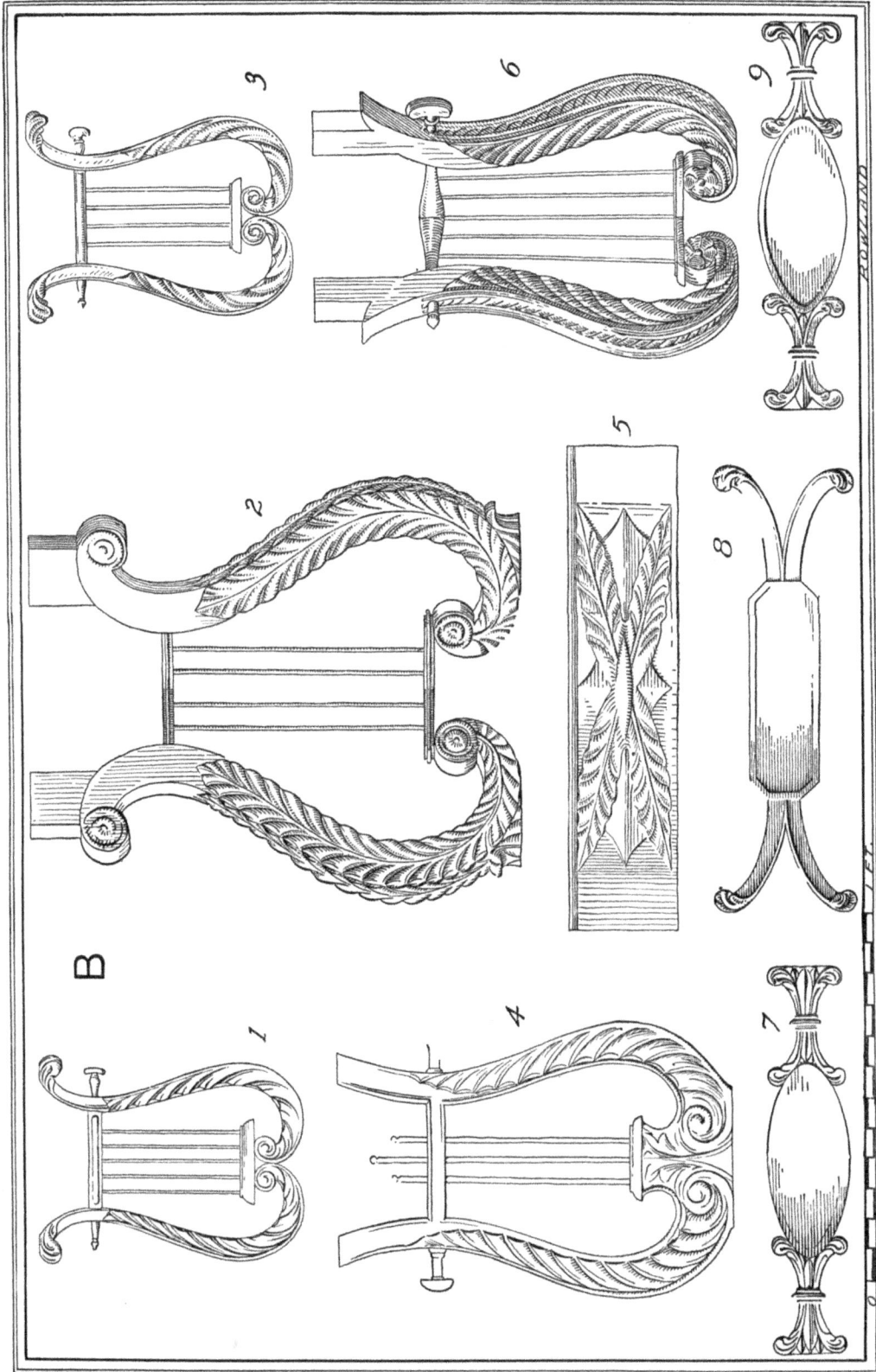

TYPICAL LYRES AND CHAIR SLATS WITH A PANEL FROM THE BASE OF A DINING-TABLE

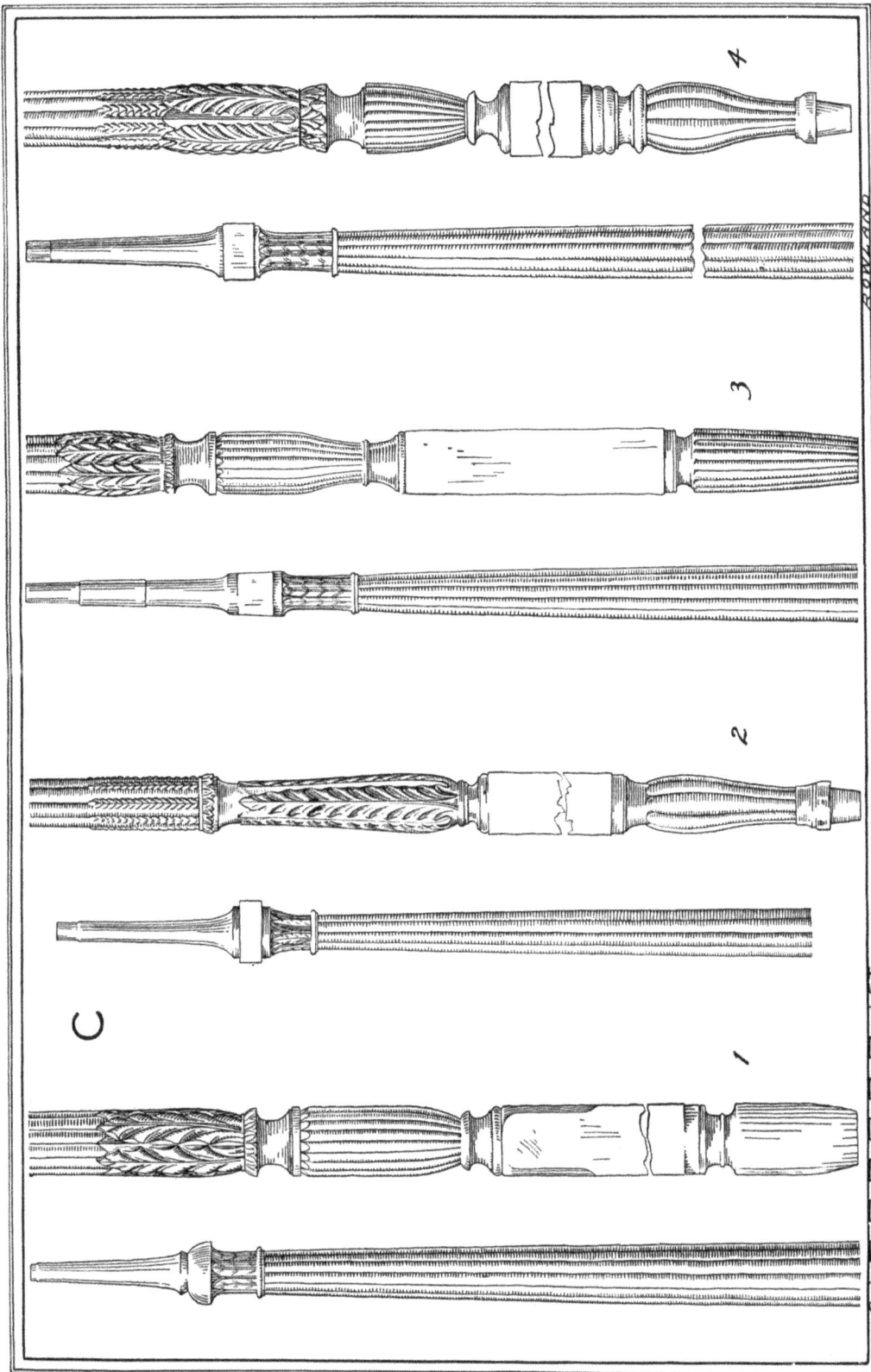

FOUR BED-POSTS

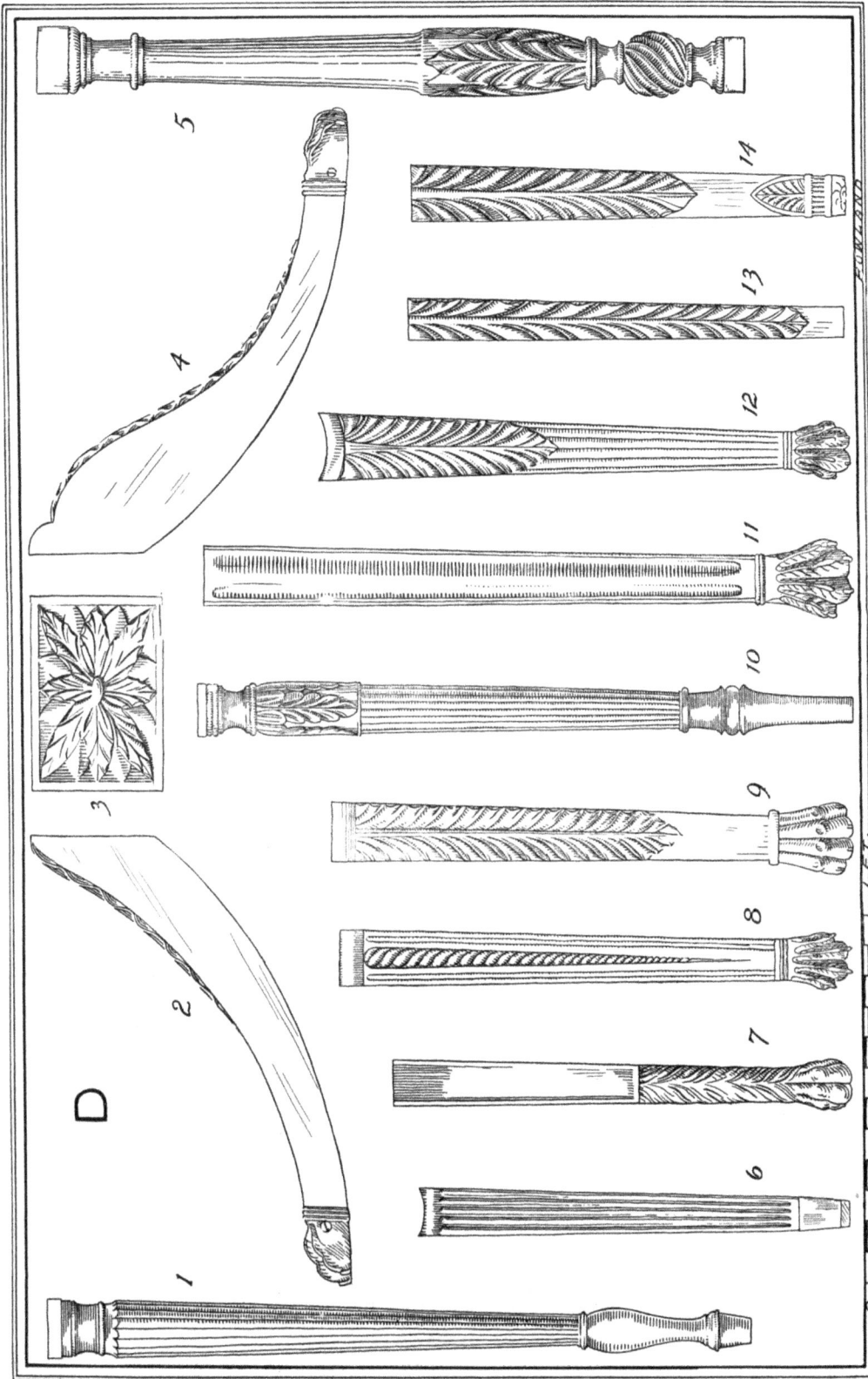

TABLE LEGS AND SUPPORTS AND A PANEL FROM A TABLE BASE

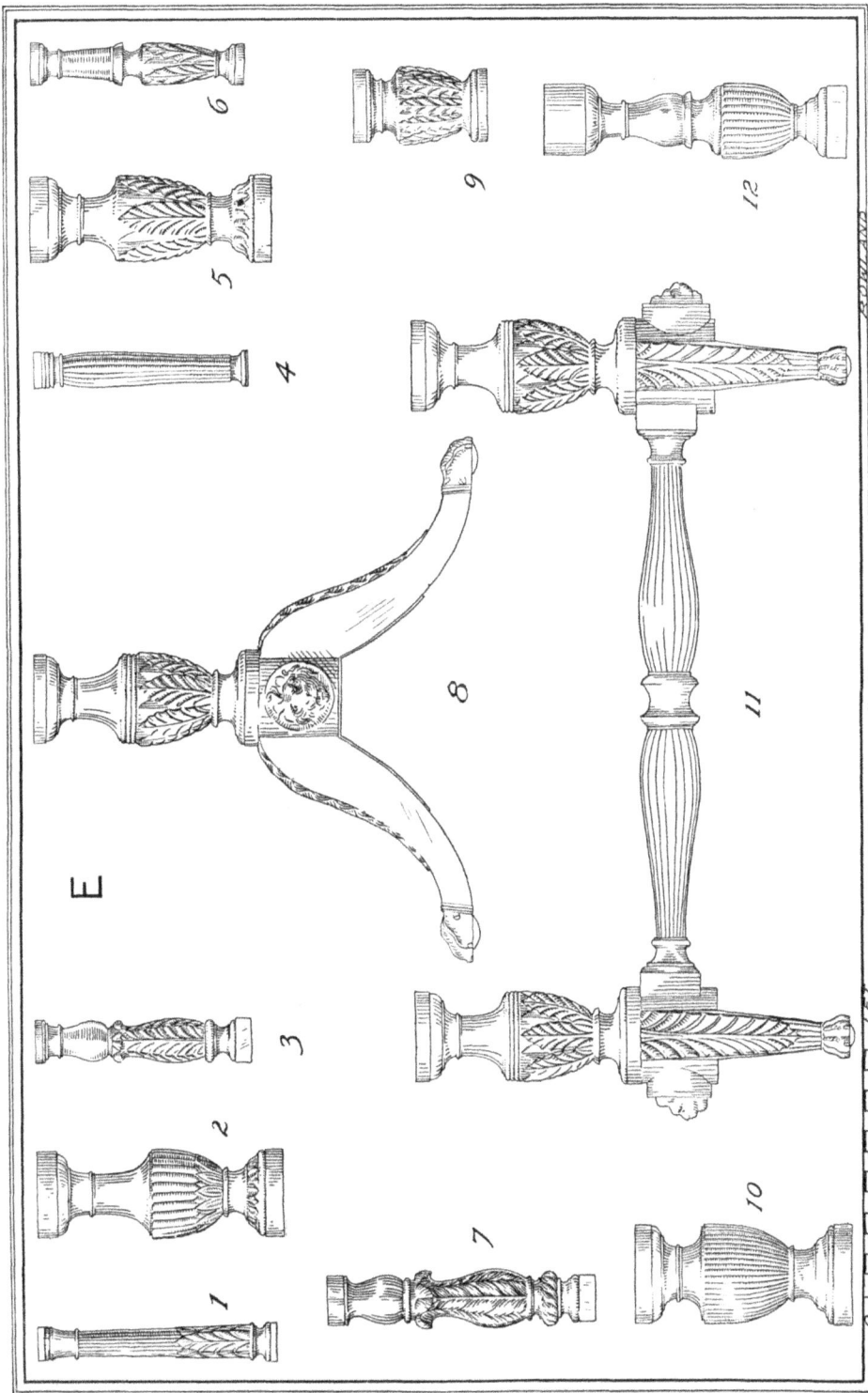

A PIANO TRESTLE AND VARIOUS DESIGNS OF TABLE POSTS AND URN-SHAPED SUPPORTS

www.ingramcontent.com/pod-product-compliance
Lightning Source LLC
Chambersburg PA
CBHW081346280326
41927CB00042B/3191